VERY
HUNGRY
GREEK

VERY HUNGRY GREEK

©2022 Christina Kynigos &
Meze Publishing Limited
First edition printed in 2022 in the UK
ISBN: 978-1-915538-25-3
Written by: Christina Kynigos
Edited by: Katie Fisher, Phil Turner
Photography by: Paul Gregory
www.paulgregoryphotography.co.uk
Designed by: Paul Cocker
PR: Emma Toogood, Lizzy Capps
Contributors: Ekta Rajagopalan, Lis Ellis,
Lizzie Morton, Radha Joshi
Printed and bound in the UK
by CPI Antony Rowe

@VeryHungryGreek

Published by Meze Publishing Limited
Unit 1b, 2 Kelham Square
Kelham Riverside
Sheffield S3 8SD
Web: www.mezepublishing.co.uk
Telephone: 0114 275 7709
Email: info@mezepublishing.co.uk

CONTENTS

BREAKFAST

LIGHTER BITES

DELICIOUS DINNERS

ONE POT WONDERS

FAKEAWAYS

STREET FOOD

SIDES & SNACKS

SWEET TREATS

MY STORY

Growing up in a Greek-Cypriot household meant one thing: big portions. I was quite a chubby kid, always hungry and loved my food right from the start. My family didn't do things by halves, mainly down to the Greek culture of being 'feeders'. Also, my Yiayia and Bapou (grandmother and grandad in Greek) would always make the most amazing food and I could never say no to having seconds. I've lived with them since I was 1, so loved watching them cook from an early age. Then I started helping them in the kitchen and my love for cooking grew, but so did my weight.

I knew I had to do something about it, so I decided to put together healthy recipes that would feel like I was eating all my favourite foods and takeaways but were much lower in calories. In the spring of 2020, I started posting my recipes on Instagram and the response was overwhelming. My recipes were being recreated left, right and centre, and knowing that I could help others on their journey while enjoying all their favourite foods made me so happy.

That's when the Very Hungry Greek was born.

ABOUT MY BOOK

This isn't your standard cookbook for healthy food, this is healthy food porn. I made this cookbook to go beyond the boundaries of what we can eat when trying to lose a few (or more!) pounds.

I've been inspired by my love of food from around the world, but also by my Greek origins. There are Greek recipes in here that have been handed down within the family, which I've slightly tweaked to make them healthier without losing the flavour.

The aim of this book is simple; I want you to flick through and see your favourite foods and cuisines that you might typically find at restaurants, takeaways and street food vendors. I'll have put my own twist on them of course, with bags of flavour, swaps to suit even the fussiest of eaters and all of them healthy enough to eat every day without feeling an ounce of guilt.

This book isn't just for people who want to lose weight, but for anyone wanting to enjoy food without worrying about their waistline. Food is there to enjoy and these recipes will help you do just that.

Healthy food will never be boring again.

Love Christina x

KEY INGREDIENTS

Aromatics

Fresh herbs, ginger, garlic, red chilli and citrus fruits like lemons and limes are brilliant for adding a zing of flavour and are used in recipes throughout this book.

Bread

Tortilla wraps and gluten-free rolls are wonderfully low in calories and anything wholemeal, which fills you up for longer, features a lot in this book. Panko breadcrumbs are something I use regularly to make an amazing crispy coating, but you can blitz toasted gluten-free or wholemeal bread to make your own if you wish.

Herbs and Spices

I'm all about food that packs a flavour punch and I don't hold back on dried seasonings. My motto is don't be shy and experiment! Sometimes I want convenience and pre-mixed seasonings are brilliant for that, so some recipes in this book include taco seasoning, chicken seasoning and tandoori spices.

Lean Protein

If you're anything like me, crispy bacon fat or chicken skin are impossible to resist. So, cut out the temptation and buy lean meat to save on a load of calories.

Low-Calorie Cooking Spray

Essential for cutting down the calories when frying food. There are normally two types to choose from: cream-based or oil-based. I opt for the 100% oil-based variety, as a small amount goes a long way and it crispens food up nicely.

paprika
ground

Low-Fat Dairy

Fat-free Greek yoghurt, reduced-fat soft cheese and semi-skimmed milk are your go-to buys for low-fat dairy products.

Pasta, Rice, Beans and Oats

Yes...all the carbs! They all have amazing filling powers, are handy to have in the cupboard, quick to rustle up and great for bulking up dishes. They are wondrously versatile!

Soy Sauce

I wanted to call out soy sauce on its own as it's such a special ingredient. Maybe it's because I have an obsession with Asian food so I use it all the time, but it adds an amazing amount of salty depth to so many recipes in this book and I genuinely can't live without it.

Stock Pots

Swap your standard stock cube to a stock pot; it sounds silly but stock pots are bursting with flavour and come in a variety of different flavours. Don't get me wrong, I do use stock cubes for a few recipes in the book as they give a certain different flavour, but for most the stock pot is the star of the show.

Please note that throughout my recipes, all oven temperatures are for a fan oven as that's what I use at home.

BREAKFAST

THE FIVE-A-DAY SMOOTHIE

5 MINUTES   SERVES 1

The bold flavours of mango and orange make the best smoothie, but I may be a tad biased as mango is my favourite fruit. Blend them together with a splash of milk and a spoonful of thick Greek yoghurt for the creamiest energising smoothie with your five a day in one hit.

PER SERVING
290 KCAL
51G CARBS
15G PROTEIN
2G FAT

250g mango, roughly diced

1 orange, peeled and diced

40ml milk

100g fat-free Greek yoghurt

Simply blitz all the ingredients in a blender and enjoy!

Swaps: Using the yoghurt and milk as your base, experiment with your favourite fruit!

OAT BREAKFAST COOKIES

5 MINUTES   8-10 MINUTES   SERVES 1

Cookies for breakfast? What is this sorcery! A great recipe to take with you on the road; the oats are super filling with a luscious, chocolate chip surprise. Need I say more?

PER SERVING
341 KCAL
46G CARBS
9G PROTEIN
15G FAT

½ medium-size banana

40g oats

10g chocolate chips

15g smooth peanut butter

15g syrup-style sweetener

¼ tsp baking powder

Mash up the banana with the back of a fork, then mix in the rest of the ingredients. Form into 4 small cookies on a lined baking tray and bake in the oven at 180°c for 8-10 minutes. Let them rest until they've firmed up before enjoying.

Tips: Make 2 large cookies if you don't fancy them small and drizzle with melted chocolate for extra deliciousness!

CHOCOLATE & RASPBERRY STUFFED ROLL-UPS

5 MINUTES   4-5 MINUTES   SERVES 2

This is basically French toast, rolled up and stuffed with Nutella and raspberries, alongside an easy raspberry sauce for dipping and drizzling. You've got to fit your five a day in somewhere, right?

PER SERVING
388 KCAL
56G CARBS
17G PROTEIN
11G FAT

2 punnets of raspberries

2 tsp icing sugar

6 small slices of bread, crusts removed

25g Nutella

30ml semi-skimmed milk

2 eggs

1 tsp sweetener

½ tsp ground cinnamon

Low-calorie cooking spray

In a small bowl, mash half of the raspberries with the icing sugar using the back of a fork, then set aside.

Using a rolling pin, roll each piece of bread to flatten it, then spread over a thin layer of Nutella and dot with a few raspberries, crushing them lightly with a fork. Roll up each slice and make sure the seam is enclosed.

In a separate bowl, whisk the milk, eggs, sweetener and cinnamon together. Working in batches, dip the roll-ups into this mixture and then transfer them to a large frying pan sprayed with low-calorie cooking spray on a medium heat. Fry for 3-4 minutes or until cooked through and nicely browned on all sides.

Serve the roll-ups with a dusting of icing sugar, more fresh raspberries and your raspberry sauce on the side for dipping and drizzling.

Tips: Use 1-2 teaspoons of butter instead of low-calorie cooking spray for a lovely golden coating!

CHOCOLATE CHIP
BANANA BREAD BAKED OATS

5 MINUTES   20 MINUTES   SERVES 1

I'm obsessed with baked oats. They fill you up for ages so you don't reach for snacks, and you can customise them however you want with whatever toppings and spreads you have in the house. This recipe makes the baked oats super fluffy and who can say no to chocolate chips?

PER SERVING
362 KCAL
50G CARBS
15G PROTEIN
11G FAT

40g oats, blended

80g fat-free Greek yoghurt

20ml semi-skimmed milk

½ banana, mashed

½ tsp baking powder

15g chocolate chips

In a small ovenproof ramekin or dish, mix all the ingredients together but keep half the chocolate chips back. Sprinkle these on top of the mixture and then bake in the oven at 180°c for 20 minutes.

Swaps: Don't like banana? Swap it for apple sauce or a whisked egg white!

BANOFFEE PIE YOGHURT POTS

5 MINUTES SERVES 2

A classic dessert that you can eat for breakfast! Fresh banana, caramel sauce and a luscious homemade vanilla yoghurt on a caramelised biscuit base, topped off with crunchy granola for a texture explosion. Perfect for those with a sweet tooth in the morning and equally good for dessert.

PER SERVING
316 KCAL
49G CARBS
15G PROTEIN
7G FAT

200g fat-free Greek yoghurt

2 tsp powdered sweetener

2 tsp vanilla essence

2 caramelised biscuits

2 small bananas

30g caramel

50g low-sugar granola

In a bowl, mix the yoghurt, sweetener and vanilla essence together well. Crumble most of the caramelised biscuits evenly into 2 glass jars or pots, then add half the yoghurt mixture to each.

Slice the bananas and place on top of the yoghurt, then drizzle over the caramel, add the remaining yoghurt mixture and top with the granola.

Finish by sprinkling the remaining caramelised biscuit crumbs over the granola and enjoy!

Swaps: Replace the yoghurt mixture with pre-brought low-fat vanilla yoghurt!

CHEESY MARMITE CRUMPET BAKE

5 MINUTES   14-16 MINUTES   SERVES 1

You either love it or hate it and I adore it. Instead of having standard buttery crumpets, try this high-protein cheesy breakfast recipe to prep you for the day.

PER SERVING
400 KCAL
49G CARBS
26G PROTEIN
12G FAT

2 crumpets

1 egg

30ml semi-skimmed milk

20g light cheddar, grated

2 tsp Marmite

15g mozzarella, shredded

First, pop your crumpets in the toaster. In a bowl, whisk the egg and milk together, mix in the grated cheddar and set aside. Spread the Marmite evenly over the toasted crumpets, and lay them in an ovenproof dish.

Pour the egg mixture over the crumpets, then scatter the mozzarella on top and in between. Oven bake at 180°c for 14-16 minutes or until cooked and then serve hot.

Swaps: Don't like Marmite? Just leave it out. I love a cheese-pull so also used mozzarella here but using cheddar by itself will taste just as good.

CHOCOLATE ORANGE PANCAKES

5-10 MINUTES   5-10 MINUTES   SERVES 1

These taste just like a dessert and no one will believe they're made from blended oats instead of flour. They'll soon be a firm favourite for the whole family!

PER SERVING
366 KCAL
34G CARBS
26G PROTEIN
14G FAT

1 egg white

1 egg, separated

100g fat-free thick Greek yoghurt

40g oats, blended

7g cacao powder

3 tsp sweetener

1 tsp orange extract

Low-calorie cooking spray

Add the egg whites to a large bowl and beat with an electric whisk until soft peaks are formed. In a separate bowl, whisk the egg yolk with the yoghurt, blended oats, cacao powder, sweetener and orange extract. Gently fold the fluffy egg whites into the yolk mixture.

Spray a pan with low-calorie cooking spray and add a heaped tablespoon of batter per pancake. Cook on a medium heat for 1-2 minutes on each side.

Serve the pancakes with a drizzle of melted chocolate and some low-fat vanilla yoghurt.

Tips: If you don't have an electric mixer, a balloon whisk will work but be prepared for your arm to ache!

SAUSAGE, CHEESE & BEAN QUESADILLA

5 MINUTES   8-10 MINUTES   SERVES 1

This was inspired by the sausage, cheese and bean melt you can buy from a certain pastry shop. An absolute winner for fussy eaters and perfect paired with a salad for a fuss-free lunch or dinner too.

PER SERVING
423 KCAL
46G CARBS
31G PROTEIN
10G FAT

1 reduced-fat pork sausage

Low-calorie cooking spray

1 tortilla wrap

180g baked beans, heated

20g light cheddar, grated

20g reduced-fat mozzarella, diced

Salt and pepper

Remove the skin from the sausage and roll the meat into 6-8 small balls. Spray a large frying pan on a medium heat with low-calorie cooking spray and fry the sausage balls for 5-6 minutes, or until cooked through. Transfer to a plate while you prepare the wrap.

Spray the same pan with more cooking spray and add the wrap. Fry for 30 seconds until the bottom of the wrap is crispy, spray the top with cooking spray and then flip the wrap over. Fry for a further 30 seconds, then add the sausage balls, hot baked beans and both cheeses on one half of the wrap.

Season the quesadilla to taste with salt and pepper, then use a spatula to fold the empty side of the wrap over the filling and gently push down to stick everything together. Fry for 30 seconds, then flip over and fry for a further minute or until the cheese has melted.

Transfer your breakfast quesadilla to a chopping board, slice in half and enjoy.

Swaps: Swap the pork for chicken or veggie sausages!

STRAWBERRY CHEESECAKE OVERNIGHT OATS

 5 MINUTES   SERVES 1

A breakfast that tastes like pudding: what a way to start your day! Minutes to make with a bit of prep the night before and seconds to devour.

PER SERVING
361 KCAL
52G CARBS
24G PROTEIN
8G FAT

40g oats

100ml milk

2 tsp sweetener

100g fat-free Greek yoghurt

40g light soft cheese

1 tsp vanilla essence

8 strawberries, diced

½ sugar-free digestive biscuit

In a jar, mix the oats, milk and sweetener together. Store this in the fridge overnight.

The next morning, mix the yoghurt, soft cheese, vanilla and half of the strawberries together in a bowl. Spoon this over the overnight oats, then top with the remaining diced strawberries. Finally, crumble over the digestive biscuit and enjoy.

Swaps: Use whatever milk you want and swap the strawberries for any fruit your heart desires!

PESTO EGG WRAP

 5 MINUTES   5 MINUTES   SERVES 1

Perfect for a speedy breakfast. Eat as is or wrap it up for on the go.

PER SERVING
330 KCAL
25G CARBS
21G PROTEIN
15G FAT

Low-calorie cooking spray

2 eggs, whisked

Salt and pepper

1 tortilla wrap

1 tbsp reduced-fat green pesto

5 cherry tomatoes, sliced

Handful of spinach, roughly sliced

20g reduced-fat mozzarella

Spray an ovenproof pan with low-calorie cooking spray and heat on high. Once the pan is piping hot, add the whisked eggs and a good pinch of salt and pepper. Cook for around 10-15 seconds, then lay the wrap on top of the egg, pressing gently down with a spatula to help it stick.

Reduce to a medium heat and cook the eggs for a minute or until they have puffed up. Spray the top of the wrap with low-calorie cooking spray and flip. Spread the pesto over the egg layer with the back of a spoon, then add the cherry tomatoes, spinach and mozzarella.

Place the pan under a hot grill for 1-2 minutes until the cheese has melted, then transfer to a plate, wrap and serve!

Swaps: Go crazy experimenting with the ingredients! Try red pesto and whatever veg you have in the fridge.

RED PESTO & BASIL SHAKSHUKA

5 MINUTES   10-12 MINUTES   SERVES 1

Shakshuka is one hell of a breakfast, and you only need one pan to make it. The eggs simmer in a delicious pesto-spiked tomato sauce, perfect for dipping your favourite bread into. Packed with veggies, this breakfast will set you up for a goal-crushing day!

PER SERVING
335 KCAL
23G CARBS
22G PROTEIN
18G FAT

Low-calorie cooking spray

¼ red onion, finely diced

2 cloves of garlic, minced

1 tin of high-quality chopped tomatoes

Salt and pepper

4-5 basil leaves, roughly torn

25g reduced-fat red pesto

2 eggs

Bread, to serve

Spray a large, lidded frying pan or skillet with low-calorie cooking spray and fry the onion and garlic for 4-5 minutes until softened. Add the chopped tomatoes, a pinch of salt and pepper and half of the basil leaves, stirring well.

Bring the sauce to a simmer and then place the pesto in small amounts around the pan. Make two wells in the sauce and crack an egg into each.

If using a skillet, oven cook the shakshuka at 180°c for 8-10 minutes, or if using a frying pan, place under a grill for 5-10 minutes on a low heat, keeping the handle out of the grill.

Scatter with the remaining basil and then serve the shakshuka with your favourite bread or toast with a lashing of butter.

Tips: Add a pinch of chilli flakes to the sauce for some lovely background heat in your shakshuka!

LIGHTER BITES

SATAY BEEF SKEWERS

10 MINUTES   5 MINUTES   SERVES 2

Super tender beef slices that literally melt in your mouth using a simple ingredient hack, coupled with an explosion of flavour from the marinade and a heavenly satay sauce.

PER SERVING
223 KCAL
10G CARBS
32G PROTEIN
6G FAT

1 rump steak

Low-calorie cooking spray

For the marinade

2 tbsp light soy sauce

1 tsp bicarbonate of soda

1 tsp curry powder

1 tsp cornflour

For the satay sauce

40ml water

25g peanut butter powder

1 tsp dark soy sauce

1 tsp sweetener

½ tsp fish sauce

If you're using wooden skewers, soak them in hot water for a few minutes while you prepare the ingredients. For the marinade, combine all the ingredients in a shallow bowl until well mixed.

Tenderise the beef with a rolling pin, then cut into wide strips against the grain. Add the beef to the marinade and leave for at least 10 minutes. While it marinates, make the satay sauce by mixing all the ingredients together in a small saucepan.

Thread the marinated beef strips onto the skewers. Spray a frying pan with low-calorie cooking spray and place on a high heat. Add the skewers to the pan and fry them for 2 minutes on each side.

Meanwhile, cook the satay sauce on a medium heat for 1-2 minutes. Add more water to loosen the sauce if required and then pour it over the skewers.

Serve the satay beef with rice, salad and a sprinkling of chopped peanuts.

TOMATO & RED PEPPER SOUP WITH GARLIC BREAD

5 MINUTES   22-24 MINUTES   SERVES 2

Roasted red pepper has the most amazing flavour and I'm addicted, so I mixed this with the sweetness of tomatoes to make the most incredible soup. If you're not a fan of garlic bread, team this up with a cheese toastie instead.

PER SERVING
290 KCAL
45G CARBS
7G PROTEIN
7G FAT

Low-calorie cooking spray

450g roasted red peppers

4 spring onions, sliced

2 cloves of garlic, sliced

1 tsp salt and pepper

1 tsp red chilli flakes

2-3 tsp paprika

1 tin of chopped tomatoes

1 litre chicken stock

1-2 tbsp finely chopped fresh coriander

40ml reduced-fat crème fraiche

For the garlic bread

2 ciabatta rolls, sliced

1 clove of garlic, peeled

2 tsp light butter or spread, melted

1 tsp finely chopped fresh parsley

Spray a large pan with low-calorie cooking spray and fry the red peppers, spring onion and garlic for 2-3 minutes. Add the seasoning and chopped tomatoes, fry for a further 5-6 minutes, then stir in the chicken stock and fresh coriander. Bring the soup to the boil and then simmer for 15 minutes.

For the garlic bread

While the soup is simmering, prepare the garlic bread by lightly toasting and rubbing a garlic clove over each half of the ciabatta rolls. In a small bowl, mix the melted butter and parsley together, then brush over the toasted bread.

Blitz the soup with a handheld stick blender then check and adjust the seasoning if needed. Serve each bowl with a dollop of the crème fraiche on top or blend it into soup for creaminess.

Tips: This soup is just as delicious without the crème fraiche, but it won't be creamy!

SWEET POTATO FALAFEL WITH GARLIC & HERB DIP

5 MINUTES   35-40 MINUTES   SERVES 4

Standard falafels are usually slightly dry in the middle with a crispy exterior, whereas these bad boys are super soft in the centre (unless you cook them for longer) because of the sweet potato texture. Melt in-the-mouth carby delight.

PER SERVING
250 KCAL
45G CARBS
10G PROTEIN
4G FAT

400g sweet potato

1 tin of chickpeas, drained

70g oat flour

1 tsp paprika

½ tsp garlic granules

½ tsp onion granules

½ tsp ground cumin

2 tbsp finely chopped fresh coriander

Squeeze of lemon juice

For the garlic & herb dip

45g natural yoghurt

1 tbsp light mayonnaise

½ tsp mixed herbs

½ tsp garlic granules

Squeeze of lemon juice

Pierce the sweet potato with a fork or skewer as many times as you can and place in the microwave for 8 minutes, turning over halfway through so it cooks evenly on each side. Discard the skin and mash the sweet potato flesh with a fork in a large bowl.

Add the chickpeas to the sweet potato and mash with a fork, then stir in the rest of the ingredients. Roll the mixture into 12-14 balls and place on a lined baking tray. Spray the falafel with low-calorie cooking spray and then oven cook at 190°c for 25-30 minutes, or until crispy on the outside and soft in the middle.

For the garlic & herb dip

Mix all the ingredients together in a small bowl, serve alongside your baked falafels and enjoy.

BATTERED CHINESE TOFU

5 MINUTES   5 MINUTES   SERVES 2

After I made this dish for the first time, I couldn't stop making it! It's so meaty you wouldn't believe that it's vegetarian and super easy to make vegan. With a sticky teriyaki glaze, this might be your new favourite meat-free dish.

PER SERVING
267 KCAL
23G CARBS
20G PROTEIN
11G FAT

280g extra firm tofu

16g cornflour

Low-calorie cooking spray

1 spring onion, diced

For the sauce

30g teriyaki sauce

1 tbsp soy sauce

1 tsp honey

1 clove of garlic, minced

2.5cm fresh ginger, minced

Mix all the ingredients for the sauce together in a bowl and set aside. Cut the tofu into 8 equal strips and coat well in the cornflour. Spray a large pan with plenty of low-calorie cooking spray and fry the tofu for 4-5 minutes. Flip the slices over halfway through and spray again until lovely and crispy.

Crank the heat up high and then add the sauce. Let it bubble for 15 seconds, then flip the tofu again until fully coated and stir in the diced spring onion.

Sprinkle with sesame seeds and serve with boiled rice and steamed veggies. Enjoy!

Tips: Use a dash of vegetable oil to get the tofu really crispy in the pan. To make this vegan, swap the honey for a plant-based liquid sweetener.

GREEK SALAD
WITH CRISPY GARLICY GNOCCHI

5 MINUTES   5 MINUTES   SERVES 2

This is not your average Greek salad. This has all the flavours and most of the ingredients of a traditional Greek salad but the crispy little pillows of garlicy gnocchi take it to the next level.

PER SERVING
317 KCAL
36G CARBS
10G PROTEIN
14G FAT

200g gnocchi

1 clove of garlic, minced

Low-calorie cooking spray

¼ red onion, sliced

½ cucumber, sliced

1 punnet of cherry tomatoes, sliced

1 tbsp olive oil

60g feta

1 tsp oregano

Squeeze of lemon juice

Pinch of salt

In a large pan, fry the gnocchi on either side with plenty of low-calorie cooking spray for 5 minutes, or until lovely and crispy. For the last minute, add the minced garlic.

In the meantime, combine the sliced ingredients in a large bowl. In another bowl, drizzle a teaspoon of the olive oil over the feta and sprinkle in the oregano.

Add the remaining oil to the bowl of salad along with the lemon juice and salt to taste. Mix well, add the gnocchi, then crumble the dressed feta on top. If you like, add a drizzle of balsamic glaze or vinegar just before serving for an extra flavour pop. Enjoy!

Tips: Kalamata olives are a lovely addition to this recipe if you're a fan!

STICKY HALLOUMI TACOS

 5-10 MINUTES   14-16 MINUTES   SERVES 2

All Greeks love halloumi and I cook with it a lot at home. These tacos have a sweet chilli and paprika glaze to make them utterly irresistible.

PER SERVING
422 KCAL
4G CARBS
19G PROTEIN
16G FAT

Low-calorie cooking spray

½ red onion, sliced

1 red pepper, sliced

1 yellow pepper, sliced

2 tsp paprika

Salt and pepper

100g halloumi, sliced

3 tbsp reduced-fat sweet chilli sauce

4 mini tortilla wraps

Fresh coriander

Spray a pan with low-calorie cooking spray over a medium-high heat. Add the sliced onion and pepper, then stir in half the paprika and season with a pinch of salt and pepper. Fry for 2-3 minutes to soften the veg and then remove it from the pan.

In the same pan, fry the halloumi for 1-2 minutes on either side before adding the remaining paprika and 2 tablespoons of the sweet chilli sauce, stirring to coat the slices. Season with salt and pepper, then fry for another few minutes on either side.

Toast the mini wraps for a few minutes in a clean pan sprayed with low-calorie cooking spray, then fill your tacos with the veg and halloumi. Drizzle on the remaining sweet chilli sauce, add a sprinkle of fresh coriander if you like and enjoy!

Tips: Turn these tacos into fajitas by using one regular-sized tortilla wrap per person. If you're feeling hungry, use more halloumi or extra tortillas!

SOUPA AVGOLEMONO

5 MINUTES   20 MINUTES   SERVES 3

This is a Greek's ultimate cure-all. Got a cold? Feeling blue? Have a headache? Make this simple and extra comforting chicken soup with eggs and lemon. My family would make this for me and my brother all the time growing up and we would always ask for seconds... sometimes thirds!

PER SERVING
343 KCAL
43G CARBS
34G PROTEIN
5G FAT

2 chicken breasts

1.4 litres good-quality chicken stock
(or use 2 stock cubes)

150g short-grain rice

1 lemon, juiced

2 eggs

Salt and pepper

In a large lidded pan, bring the chicken breasts in the chicken stock to the boil. Simmer for 10-12 minutes until the chicken is cooked through, then remove it and pour the rice into the stock. Stir briefly, then simmer with the lid on for 10-15 minutes or until the rice is tender.

Meanwhile, whisk the lemon juice and eggs together in a large bowl. Gradually add 4-5 ladles of hot stock to the lemony eggs while whisking continuously, pouring slowly so the mixture doesn't curdle. Asking someone in your household to ladle the stock in for you makes this a lot easier!

Slowly stir the egg mixture into the pan of rice and stock. Season with a good pinch of salt and pepper to taste, then shred the cooked chicken and mix it in.

Once the soup is served, add a bit more black pepper and another squeeze of lemon juice on top. Dip crusty bread into your soup for a match made in heaven.

Tips: Normally you boil the chicken for at least an hour to create an amazing stock but following my cheat method above, you can make this soup in no time at all. Not in a hurry? Make your own chicken stock instead!

LAMB KOFTA PITTA WITH MINTED YOGHURT SAUCE

 5 MINUTES 10 MINUTES SERVES 3

A Middle Eastern classic: spiced ground lamb wrapped around wooden skewers in a warm pitta. While they're being grilled, these will fill your house with the most amazing aromas!

PER SERVING
299 KCAL
25G CARBS
22G PROTEIN
10G FAT

For the minted yoghurt sauce

100g fat-free natural yoghurt

Squeeze of lemon juice

1 tsp mint sauce

For the kofta

250g reduced-fat lamb mince

2 cloves of garlic, minced

2 tbsp finely diced fresh parsley

1 tsp ground cumin

1 tsp paprika

½ tsp salt

½ tsp black pepper

To serve

6 wooden skewers

3 pitta breads

Mixed salad

Soak the wooden skewers in water for a few minutes. Mix the ingredients for the minted yoghurt sauce together and place in the fridge.

Combine the ingredients for the kofta using your hands until well mixed, then divide into 6 equal pieces. Shape the meat around the soaked skewers and place on a lined baking tray.

Grill the kofta for 8-10 minutes, flipping them over halfway through, or until cooked. Sliding them carefully off the skewers, place 1 or 2 lamb koftas into each pitta along with some salad and a drizzle of the minted yoghurt sauce. Enjoy!

MEATBALL MARINARA SUB

5 MINUTES   20-22 MINUTES   SERVES 2

Big juicy meatballs smothered in rich marinara sauce: it's time to get seriously messy
but it'll be totally worth it.

PER SERVING
461 KCAL
3G CARBS
43G PROTEIN
16G FAT

250g lean beef mince

½ onion, finely diced

Low-calorie cooking spray

100ml beef stock

250g passata

1 tbsp tomato purée

1 tsp dried oregano

2-3 drops of Worcestershire sauce

2 gluten-free rolls, sliced

50g reduced-fat cheddar, grated

40g mozzarella, grated

Combine the beef mince and diced onion in a large bowl, then form the mixture into 8 meatballs of equal size. Spray a large frying pan with low-calorie cooking spray and fry the meatballs on a medium heat for 8-10 minutes. Meanwhile, lightly toast the rolls under the grill or in another pan.

After this time, pour half the beef stock into the pan and stir to coat each meatball with the stock for a few minutes. Remove the meatballs, pour in the passata and remaining stock, then add the purée, oregano and Worcestershire sauce to the pan. Mix well and leave on a medium heat to reduce for 8-10 minutes.

Place the meatballs back into the marinara sauce, coating them well, then divide them between the lightly toasted rolls with a ladle of marinara sauce over each. Sprinkle over the cheeses and place under a hot grill until the cheese has melted.

Serve your sub with fresh rocket inside and enjoy.

FIRECRACKER SALMON POKE BOWL

5 MINUTES   7-8 MINUTES   SERVES 2

I'm not kidding you when I say that after first developing this recipe, I ate it for lunch every day of the week. This is a sushi roll in a bowl with a ton of flavour.

PER SERVING
418 KCAL
41G CARBS
27G PROTEIN
17G FAT

2 salmon fillets

Low-calorie cooking spray

200g cooked rice

2 tsp sriracha

2 tsp soy sauce

2 tbsp light mayonnaise

Pinch of furikake seasoning (optional)

For the marinade

1 small red chilli, finely diced

2 tbsp soy sauce

2 tsp sriracha

2 tsp reduced-sugar sweet chilli
sauce

2 tsp finely chopped fresh coriander

1 tsp fish sauce

For the salad

1 carrot, grated

5cm cucumber, diced

2 spring onions, sliced

Place all the ingredients for the marinade in a bowl and coat the salmon fillets, then leave them to marinate for at least 20 minutes.

Fry the marinated salmon with low-calorie cooking spray in a pan on a medium heat for 6-7 minutes, or until cooked through.

Arrange the rice and salad in the serving bowls, then place the cooked salmon on top and drizzle with the sriracha, soy sauce and mayonnaise. If you like, add a sprinkle of furikake seasoning to finish.

BAHN MI

5-10 MINUTES   4-5 MINUTES   SERVES 2

A Vietnamese baguette with a whole lot of character. Beautifully tender soy and lemongrass pork with pickled vegetables and a pop of freshness from coriander leaves and cucumber, all served in a crispy baguette. The contrast of textures and flavours will really blow your mind!

PER SERVING
449 KCAL
47G CARBS
25G PROTEIN
17G FAT

200g lean pork loin

2 baguettes (120g)

2 tbsp light mayonnaise

2-3 sprigs of fresh coriander

4-6 cucumber ribbons or thin slices

For the pickle

1 tbsp maple syrup

2 tbsp rice vinegar

4-6 carrot ribbons or thin slices

For the marinade

2.5cm fresh ginger, minced

1 clove of garlic, minced

2 tbsp soy sauce

1 tbsp honey

1 tsp lemongrass paste

½ tsp fish sauce

For the pickle

Simply combine the ingredients in a bowl and set aside.

For the marinade

Combine the ingredients in another bowl ready for the pork.

Flatten the pork with the back of a rolling pin or tenderiser, then slice it thinly at an angle. Marinate the pork for as long as possible as the longer you leave it, the more tender it becomes.

Meanwhile, if the baguette isn't crispy, toast in the oven at 180°c for a few minutes, then set aside.

Fry the pork in a pan for 4-5 minutes on a medium heat or until cooked. Slice the baguette horizontally in half without cutting all the way through, then spread each side with mayonnaise. Add a layer of cooked pork, pickled veg, plenty of coriander and cucumber ribbons. Go crazy and use as much or little as you want.

Serve with a drizzle of sriracha, more mayonnaise and a few sliced red chillies for a lovely kick.

Tips: I love using the bake at home baguettes in this recipe for extra crispiness!

KEFTEDES

5 MINUTES   8-10 MINUTES   SERVES 2

Greek meatballs are juicy, tender and beautifully flavoured. Traditionally they're fried, but my way reduces the calories and doesn't compromise on flavour. A great accompaniment for a meze, as a main meal served with Greek salad or a protein-rich snack.

PER SERVING
295 KCAL
4G CARBS
45G PROTEIN
11G FAT

½ medium onion, grated

1 clove of garlic, minced

200g pork mince

200g beef mince

1 egg

3 tbsp finely diced fresh parsley

1 tbsp finely diced fresh mint

½ tsp baking powder

½ tsp ground cinnamon

Salt and pepper

Squeeze of lemon juice

Using a paper towel, squeeze the juice out of the grated onion and then tip the onion into a large bowl. Add the rest of the ingredients and mix well using your hands. If you're not short on time, let the mixture rest in the fridge for 30 minutes at this stage to firm up.

Roll the mixture into 12 balls, place them on a lined baking tray and grill for 8-10 minutes, turning carefully halfway through.

Serve with a Greek salad (see my recipe on page 56) and enjoy!

DELICIOUS DINNERS

CHICKEN PARMIGIANO PASTA BAKE

5 MINUTES   10-15 MINUTES   SERVES 4

Deliciously crispy breaded chicken breasts, smothered in a homemade tomato sauce, topped with a lashing of gooey mozzarella. Oh, and the best part? Made into a pasta bake. A winning dish for meal prepping.

PER SERVING
448 KCAL
52G CARBS
40G PROTEIN
8G FAT

2 chicken breasts

20g parmesan, grated

40g panko breadcrumbs

1 egg, whisked

Low-calorie cooking spray

200g penne pasta, just cooked

160g reduced-fat mozzarella, shredded

Handful of basil leaves, finely chopped

For the sauce

2 cloves of garlic, minced

500g passata

40g tomato purée

1 tsp Italian herbs

½ tsp onion granules

½ tsp garlic granules

Pinch of salt and pepper

Butterfly the chicken breasts then slice through so you've got 4 flat pieces. Mix the parmesan and panko breadcrumbs together in a shallow bowl and whisk the egg in another. Dip the chicken pieces into the whisked egg, then the breadcrumbs. Fry in a large pan with some low-calorie cooking spray on a medium heat for 2 minutes on either side.

For the sauce

Remove the crumbed chicken, then in the same pan on a medium heat with a little more cooking spray, fry the garlic for 1 minute. Add all the remaining ingredients and cook on a medium heat for 1-2 minutes.

In an ovenproof dish, layer up the cooked pasta and breadcrumbed chicken, then spoon over the tomato sauce. Top with the mozzarella and cook in the oven at 180°c for 12-14 minutes or until the cheese is golden and the chicken is cooked through. Scatter over the fresh basil, serve with a large salad and enjoy!

Swaps: Make sure you cook the pasta for 3 minutes less than usual so it doesn't overcook in the oven. Mixed herbs or oregano would also work instead of Italian herbs.

GNOCCHI BOLOGNESE

🍳 5-10 MINUTES   🍲 20-22 MINUTES   🍽 SERVES 3

A whopping four out of your five a day, and you may even have leftovers for the next day!
Pillowy-soft gnocchi in a beefy Bolognese with lots of gooey cheesy goodness.
You could also pan-fry instead of boiling the gnocchi with plenty of cooking spray to
make them nice and crispy for a lovely bite!

PER SERVING
459 KCAL
58G CARBS
32G PROTEIN
9G FAT

Low-calorie cooking spray

1 onion, finely diced

1 pepper, finely diced

6 mushrooms, finely diced

250g beef mince

500g passata

1 tin of chopped tomatoes

2 beef stock cubes

1 tsp mixed herbs

½ tsp black pepper

400g gnocchi, boiled

50g reduced-fat cheddar, grated

In a large pan sprayed with low-calorie cooking spray, fry the veg for 3-4 minutes to soften, then add the mince and brown for a further 3-4 minutes. Mix in the rest of the ingredients except the gnocchi and cheese, then cook the sauce for a further 10-12 minutes or until thickened.

Mix in the gnocchi, cover with the cheese and place under a hot grill until the topping has melted. Serve with a sprinkle of dried parsley on top and garlic bread alongside.

Tips: Don't fancy gnocchi? Swap it for cooked pasta!

KING PRAWN LAKSA

5 MINUTES   18-20 MINUTES   SERVES 2

Laksa is basically the vibrant flavours of a red Thai curry in a creamy coconut broth with noodles.
It's delicious and probably the most fragrant dish I've ever eaten!

PER SERVING

427 KCAL
35G CARBS
36G PROTEIN
8G FAT

Low-calorie cooking spray

1 red pepper, finely diced

1 spring onion, diced

1 red chilli, finely diced

2 cloves of garlic, minced

50g Thai red curry paste

200ml reduced-fat coconut milk

10g peanut butter powder

1 tsp sweetener

100g dried egg noodles

180g raw king prawns

600ml vegetable stock

½ lime, zested and juiced

3 sprigs of fresh coriander, chopped

In a pan sprayed with low-calorie cooking spray, fry the pepper, spring onion, chilli and garlic for a few minutes to soften them.

Add the Thai curry paste to the vegetables and fry for a further minute to release the flavours, then add the coconut milk, peanut butter powder and sweetener.

Bring to the boil then reduce to a simmer. Add the noodles, king prawns and vegetable stock to simmer for 6-7 minutes until cooked through.

Add the lime zest and juice to the pan, then serve with a sprinkle of fresh coriander and enjoy!

CHEESE & BROCCOLI ALFREDO

5 MINUTES   16-18 MINUTES   SERVES 2

A delicious, super quick veggie dish that skips the heavy cream and replaces it with even more cheese. Creamy cheesy broccoli goodness that's great for meal prepping.

PER SERVING
387 KCAL
57G CARBS
20G PROTEIN
9G FAT

½ onion, finely diced

Low-calorie cooking spray

1 tsp Italian seasoning

Salt and pepper

215g vegetable stock

140g penne pasta

30ml semi-skimmed milk

50g light cheddar

1 tbsp parmesan, grated

8 broccoli florets, cooked

In a saucepan, fry the onion in low-calorie cooking spray for 2-3 minutes to soften, then stir in the Italian seasoning and a good pinch of salt and pepper.

Pour over the vegetable stock and add the pasta to the pan. Cook on a low heat with the lid on for 10-12 minutes until the pasta is cooked and the water has been absorbed.

Mix in the milk and cheeses for 1-2 minutes, or until the pasta is lovely and creamy. Stir in the cooked broccoli and enjoy.

CHICKEN & PESTO LASAGNE

5 MINUTES   25-30 MINUTES   SERVES 4

A twist on an Italian classic. I'm a huge fan of pesto, I'd say I'm a little obsessed! Team it up with chicken, spinach and a beautifully creamy bechamel sauce for a match made in heaven.

PER SERVING
444 KCAL
29G CARBS
35G PROTEIN
20G FAT

15g light butter

15g plain flour

250ml semi-skimmed milk

40g parmesan, grated

70g green pesto

280g cooked chicken, sliced

5 balls of frozen spinach, thawed

6 lasagne sheets

100g mozzarella, shredded

To make the bechamel sauce, heat up the butter in a pan and add the flour. Mix well to create a paste and cook on a medium heat for a further 1-2 minutes. Gradually add the milk, whisking well, until it starts to thicken. Continue stirring and cooking gently until you've used up all the milk and the bechamel has thickened.

Add the parmesan and pesto to the bechamel sauce, mix well until the cheese has melted and then stir in the cooked chicken and thawed spinach.

Now build your lasagne in an ovenproof dish. Put a small amount of the bechamel sauce on the bottom, cover it with 3 of the lasagne sheets, top with half the chicken mixture, then repeat. Top your lasagne with the shredded mozzarella, cover the dish with foil and oven cook at 220°c for 20 minutes. Remove the foil and cook for a further 5 minutes or until the cheese is golden.

Serve with a large salad and enjoy!

Swaps: You can use cooked chicken thighs, breasts or rotisserie chicken for this recipe. For the sauce, light spread like margarine instead of butter works too!

PHILLY CHEESESTEAK
STUFFED PASTA SHELLS

10 MINUTES   20 MINUTES   SERVES 4

While Philly Cheesesteak is traditionally served in a baguette and originated in the US, I fancied an Italian twist on this American classic. The pasta shells are stuffed with wonderfully seasoned beef mince, diced veg and a glorious layer of melted cheddar cheese.

PER SERVING
418 KCAL
49G CARBS
32G PROTEIN
10G FAT

Low-calorie cooking spray

1 onion, finely diced

350g lean beef mince

1 red pepper, finely diced

1 green pepper, finely diced

200ml beef stock

2 tsp Worcestershire sauce

2 tbsp reduced-fat tomato ketchup

Salt and pepper

230g large pasta shells, cooked

80g light cheddar, grated

In a large pan lightly coated with low-calorie cooking spray, soften the onion for 2-3 minutes, then add the mince to brown for a further 2-3 minutes. Stir in the diced peppers, beef stock, Worcestershire sauce and tomato ketchup along with a good pinch of salt and pepper to taste.

Fry the mince mixture for 10-12 minutes or until all the liquid has been absorbed and the veg has softened. Place a heaped teaspoon of this filling into each pasta shell and line them up in an ovenproof dish. Fill up the pasta shells with any remaining mince, then sprinkle the grated cheese evenly over the top.

Place the dish under a hot grill for a few minutes or until the cheese has melted, then serve with a handful of mixed leaves.

Tips: Make this creamier and more indulgent with a bechamel sauce poured into the dish before you place the pasta shells on top!

VEGGIE SINGAPORE NOODLES

5 MINUTES   8 MINUTES   SERVES 2

A healthy twist on a takeaway dish using thin vermicelli noodles cooked in minutes, coated in curry powder and soy sauce for tons of flavour, and all the veg you can whack into it. It's brilliant if you have veg to use up, eaten on its own or as a side with your fakeaway.

PER SERVING
255 KCAL
51G CARBS
9G PROTEIN
1G FAT

100g dried vermicelli noodles

Low-calorie cooking spray

½ onion, sliced

1 red pepper, sliced

1 spring onion, sliced

1 packet of mangetout, sliced

2.5cm fresh ginger, minced

1 clove of garlic, minced

2 tsp curry powder

1 tbsp soy sauce

1 tsp sweetener

Soak the vermicelli noodles in boiling water for 1 minute, drain and then rinse under cold running water.

Spray a large wok or pan with low-calorie cooking spray and fry the onion for 2-3 minutes or until softened. Add the rest of the veg, ginger and garlic and stir fry for a further few minutes.

Add the prepared noodles to the pan along with the curry powder, soy sauce and sweetener. Mix well and then serve straight away. This goes very well with my homemade gyozas on page 202.

Tips: This is delicious with cooked prawns, chicken pieces or tofu for an added protein hit!

KOREAN 'FRIED' CHICKEN

10 MINUTES • 15-20 MINUTES • SERVES 2

This tastes so naughty that I can't quite believe it's so low in calories! I mimicked the crispy coating without the need for frying and made an incredibly sticky Korean sauce to coat the cooked chicken.

PER SERVING
347 KCAL
27G CARBS
45G PROTEIN
6G FAT

2 chicken breasts, diced

Salt and pepper

1 clove of garlic, minced

2.5cm fresh ginger, minced

1 tbsp soy sauce

1 egg

30g cornflour

Low-calorie cooking spray

Sesame seeds, to garnish

Spring onion, finely diced

For the sauce

25g gochujang paste

2.5cm fresh ginger, minced

2 tbsp reduced-sugar tomato ketchup

2 tbsp water

1 tbsp soy sauce

1 tsp sesame oil

1 tsp sweetener

1 tsp honey

Season the diced chicken breast with a pinch of salt and pepper, then coat in the garlic, ginger and soy sauce. Set aside for at least 10 minutes to marinate. Meanwhile, mix all the ingredients for the sauce together and set aside.

Crack the egg into a shallow bowl and whisk, then put the cornflour into another bowl. Dip the marinated chicken in the whisked egg and then the cornflour to coat each piece. Place on a lined baking tray, cover generously with low-calorie cooking spray and oven cook at 180°c for 15 minutes, or until the chicken is done.

Transfer the sauce to a large saucepan and cook on a high heat for 1 minute, or until it starts to bubble. Add the cooked chicken and coat well.

Sprinkle with the sesame seeds and finely diced spring onion, then serve with cooked rice.

Tips: Want to feed 4 people instead of 2? Double up on all the ingredients apart from the egg. Want it spicier? Add more gochujang paste to your sauce.

MELT-IN-THE-MIDDLE FISHCAKES

10 MINUTES   24-28 MINUTES   SERVES 2

I used to eat fishcakes all the time when I was little. My grandparents owned a fish and chip shop (obviously, what Greek hasn't?!) and would always make the freshest fishcakes so I got inspired by them. I've added my own twist though with a cheesy protein-filled centre.

PER SERVING
338 KCAL
37G CARBS
42G PROTEIN
3G FAT

3 small haddock fillets (240g in total)

1 potato, diced and boiled

2 large sprigs of fresh parsley, finely diced

1 spring onion, diced

1 tsp onion granules

Salt and pepper

40g light cheddar cheese

25g panko breadcrumbs

Low-calorie cooking spray

Wrap the haddock fillets in foil and oven bake at 180°c for 18-20 minutes or until cooked. Combine the cooked fish and potato in a bowl, breaking them up into small chunks with a fork.

Add the parsley, spring onion and onion granules to the bowl and mix well. Season with salt and pepper, then gently form the mixture into 4 evenly sized patties.

Cut the cheese into 4 cubes of 10g each and press one into the centre of each patty, making sure the cheese is covered. Coat each fishcake evenly with the panko breadcrumbs, gently patting the coating into the fishcake to ensure it sticks. Pop the fishcakes into the freezer for at least 5 minutes to firm them up.

Spray a pan with low-calorie cooking spray and place on a medium heat. Add the chilled fishcakes to the pan and fry for 3-4 minutes, then spray them with more low-calorie cooking spray, flip over and cook for a further 3-4 minutes until golden.

Serve with peas, chips and tartare sauce.

Tips: These can be cooked in the oven or an air fryer too!

BEEF STROGANOFF PIE

5-10 MINUTES   26-28 MINUTES   SERVES 2

A creamy beefy gravy flavoured with mustard and mushrooms, topped with filo pastry for an amazing crunch. A serious texture sensation.

PER SERVING
379 KCAL
31G CARBS
39G PROTEIN
10G FAT

Low-calorie cooking spray

1 onion, sliced

2 cloves of garlic, minced

6 mushrooms, sliced

1 tin of beef consommé

1 beef stock cube

1 tbsp tomato purée

1 tsp English mustard

2-3 tsp paprika

245g rump steak, tenderised

Salt and pepper

45g crème fraiche

2 tbsp finely chopped fresh parsley

A few sheets of filo pastry

In a large frying pan coated with low-calorie cooking spray, fry the onion on a low-medium heat for 5-7 minutes to soften, then add the garlic and mushrooms. Fry for a further minute then add the consommé, stock cube, tomato purée, mustard and paprika. Simmer the sauce for 12-14 minutes.

Meanwhile, spray the steak with low-calorie cooking spray and rub in well, then season with a good pinch of salt and pepper. Fry in a very hot, dry pan (it needs to sizzle as soon as the steak touches it!) for 2 minutes on either side over a high heat, then leave to rest for a few minutes.

Mix the crème fraiche into the sauce, then thinly slice the rested beef and stir it in along with the parsley. Transfer the mixture into 2 small pie dishes or 1 medium-size dish and then slightly crumble the filo pastry in your hands over the filling to top the pies.

Spray the pastry with low-calorie cooking spray and oven cook at 180°c for 8-10 minutes or until lightly golden.

Swaps: Add more crème fraiche for a creamier sauce and omit the filo to serve the stroganoff with rice instead!

SWEDISH MEATBALLS

 5-10 MINUTES   10 MINUTES   SERVES 2

My heavenly Swedish Meatballs recipe is the homemade version of the iconic Ikea meatballs and a hell of a lot easier than assembling flat-pack furniture! Super soft and juicy meatballs bathed in a creamy gravy. This is absolutely to die for.

PER SERVING
385 KCAL
15G CARBS
48G PROTEIN
14G FAT

4 reduced-fat pork sausages

200g beef mince

Low-calorie cooking spray

1 packet of tenderstem broccoli

300ml beef stock

1 tsp Dijon mustard

½ tsp Worcestershire sauce

70g half-fat crème fraiche

1 tsp cornflour, mixed to a loose paste with water

Deskin the sausages and put the meat into a bowl, then add the beef mince. Combine the mixture and then shape into 14 meatballs. Spray a pan with low-calorie cooking spray and fry the meatballs on a medium heat for 7-8 minutes. Meanwhile, cook the broccoli in a pan of boiling water.

Set the meatballs aside before adding the stock, mustard and Worcestershire sauce to the pan. Mix well before stirring in the crème fraiche. Cook on a high heat for 30 seconds before adding the cornflour paste.

Now add the meatballs back to the pan, coating them in the sauce. Serve with boiled broccoli and buttery mash.

FISH & CHIP SANDWICH

5-10 MINUTES   14-16 MINUTES   SERVES 2

Your favourite chippy order, all in this ultimate sandwich. Toasted ciabatta with layers of mushy peas, salty vinegary chips and crispy panko-coated fish, all finished off with a lashing of homemade tartare sauce. The perfect way to eat it is using both hands and diving straight in.

PER SERVING
403 KCAL
62G CARBS
23G PROTEIN
6G FAT

For the tartare sauce

3 tbsp light mayonnaise

2 tsp finely chopped fresh dill or parsley

1 gherkin, diced

Squeeze of lemon juice

For the fish

120g cod fillet

1 egg, whisked

20g panko breadcrumbs

2 tsp finely chopped fresh dill

Pinch of salt and pepper

Low-calorie cooking spray

For the chips

200g chips, cooked

1 tsp malt vinegar

½ tsp salt

To serve

2 gluten-free ciabatta rolls

200g mushy peas, heated

For the tartare sauce, combine all the ingredients in a small bowl and place in the fridge.

For the fish, slice the cod fillet into 4 pieces. Put the egg in one bowl and the panko breadcrumbs mixed with the dill and seasoning in another. Dip the fish into the egg and then the breadcrumb coating until completely covered. Place on a lined baking tray and spray with plenty of low-calorie cooking spray, then oven cook the fish at 200°c for 14-16 minutes, or until cooked through.

Season the hot chips with the salt and vinegar, adding more or less to taste. Slice the ciabatta rolls open and toast them, then assemble the sandwiches with a layer of warm mushy peas on the bottom half, a stack of chips, half the breaded fish, then some tartare sauce. Or any other way your heart desires!

Tips: Any white fish will do here, I normally go with haddock or cod.

ONE POT WONDERS

CHEESEBURGER MAC & CHEESE

5 MINUTES 15 MINUTES SERVES 2

Before I tried this dish for the first time, I thought that anything tasting like a cheeseburger should include bread, right? How wrong I was. This has all the great flavours of a scrumptious burger and is one of the most loved recipes on my blog.

PER SERVING
450 KCAL
43G CARBS
35G PROTEIN
15G FAT

200g macaroni, cooked

30g light spreadable cheese

Low-calorie cooking spray

½ onion, finely diced

200g lean beef mince

1 beef stock cube

1 tbsp tomato purée

1 tsp oregano

½ tsp English mustard

½ tsp garlic granules

Black pepper

50g light cheddar cheese, grated

2 gherkins, sliced

1 tbsp burger sauce

Drain the pasta but keep a tablespoon of the cooking water aside. Mix the spreadable cheese into the hot pasta until melted, using the reserved pasta water if needed. You shouldn't need any heat but keep it on low if needed.

In a large frying pan with some low-calorie cooking spray, fry the onion on a medium heat for 4-5 minutes until softened, then add the mince and fry for 4-5 minutes or until cooked through. Dissolve the beef stock cube in a few tablespoons of boiling water and mix this into the mince.

Add the tomato purée, oregano, mustard, garlic granules and black pepper to the pan. Stir well, then fold the cheesy pasta into the mince mixture. Sprinkle the grated cheddar over the top, then stick under a hot grill until the cheese has melted.

Top your mac and cheese with the sliced gherkins and a drizzle of burger sauce, then enjoy.

PERI PERI CHICKEN ORZO

5 MINUTES   15-20 MINUTES   SERVES 4

This is a great dish to use up any remaining veg in your house. The peri peri seasoning gives it a lovely little kick and, of course, goes brilliantly with chicken.

PER SERVING
412 KCAL
52G CARBS
41G PROTEIN
4G FAT

2 tbsp + 1 tsp peri peri seasoning

3 chicken breasts, diced

Low-calorie cooking spray

1 red pepper, finely diced

1 yellow pepper, finely diced

1 orange pepper, finely diced

8 cherry tomatoes, sliced

200g orzo

500g passata

500ml chicken stock

Sprigs of flat leaf parsley

Massage 1 tablespoon of the peri peri seasoning into the diced chicken, then in a lidded pan coated with low-calorie cooking spray, fry the chicken on a medium-high heat for 2 minutes either side.

Add the peppers and cherry tomatoes, cook for a further 2-3 minutes to soften, then add the orzo, passata, stock and remaining peri peri seasoning to the pan. Mix well and cook with the lid on for 12-15 minutes or until all the liquid has been absorbed by the pasta.

Stir occasionally to stop it from sticking and once ready, serve with a sprinkle of fresh parsley.

Tips: This is a perfect way to use up any veg in the house and great for meal prepping!

CHICKEN CALABRESE

5 MINUTES   16-18 MINUTES   SERVES 2

Inspired by a visit to one of my favourite Italian restaurants in Leamington Spa,
I knew I had to recreate my own low-calorie version of this dish: pan-fried chicken thighs
in a passata sauce, with crispy potatoes and cherry tomatoes, finished off with harissa,
crème fraiche and melted mozzarella.

PER SERVING
375 KCAL
3G CARBS
29G PROTEIN
15G FAT

1 potato

Low-calorie cooking spray

2 boneless chicken thighs

Salt and pepper

2 tsp Italian seasoning

12 cherry tomatoes

1 red pepper, finely diced

150g passata

1 tbsp harissa paste

1 heaped tbsp reduced-fat crème fraiche

80g reduced-fat mozzarella

Pierce the potato all over with a skewer or sharp knife, microwave it for 2 minutes 30 seconds, then turn over and microwave for another 2 minutes 30 seconds. Chop into roasties, spray a large skillet or frying pan with low-calorie cooking spray and then cook the potato over a high heat for a few minutes, turning often to crisp up all sides.

Remove the potato from the pan and add the chicken thighs, seasoned with salt, pepper and 1 teaspoon of the Italian seasoning. Move the chicken to one side and add the cherry tomatoes and red pepper, then season with more salt and pepper. Stir in the passata along with the remaining Italian seasoning.

Cook over a medium heat for 7-8 minutes until the chicken is nearly done. Give everything a good stir, then add small dollops of the harissa and crème fraiche along with pieces of mozzarella around the pan.

Place the calabrese under a hot grill for a few minutes, or until the cheese has melted, and enjoy.

Swaps: Use nduja instead of harissa paste and mascarpone instead of crème fraiche!

SKILLET PASTITSIO

 5 MINUTES 20-25 MINUTES SERVES 3

Traditionally, pastitsio or 'pasta in the oven' includes a super-duper thick layer of bechamel mixed with eggs but with my cheat recipe you can make it in half the time, with one pan and a third less calories. I like to enjoy those saved calories in a sweet treat after the meal!

PER SERVING
448 KCAL
48G CARBS
37G PROTEIN
11G FAT

Low-calorie cooking spray

½ onion, finely diced

1 clove of garlic, minced

250g beef mince

300ml beef stock

250g passata

1 tin of chopped tomatoes

150g dry penne pasta

1 tsp dried oregano

½ tsp ground cinnamon

Salt and pepper

For the topping

30g parmesan, grated

100g reduced-fat mozzarella, shredded or grated

Spray a skillet or ovenproof pan with low-calorie cooking spray and fry the onion for 2-3 minutes to soften. Add the minced garlic and beef, then fry for a further few minutes to brown. Add the rest of the ingredients including a pinch of salt and pepper to taste, mix well, then to bring to the boil.

Once boiling, turn down the heat to a simmer for 15 minutes or until the pasta is cooked and the liquid has been absorbed.

Give the beef mixture a good stir, then top with the grated parmesan and mozzarella. Place the skillet under a hot grill until the cheese has melted and then enjoy.

BUTTERNUT SQUASH & BACON BAKE

5-10 MINUTES   25-30 MINUTES   SERVES 4

What really makes this dish special is the punch of smoky bacon flavour that goes wonderfully with the butternut squash and parmesan. You can either serve this vegetable bake with couscous or as a side to a main meal.

PER SERVING
164 KCAL
18G CARBS
13G PROTEIN
5G FAT

500g butternut squash

Low-calorie cooking spray

Salt and pepper, to taste

2 tsp paprika

6 smoked bacon medallions

40g parmesan cheese, grated

1 tbsp finely chopped fresh coriander

Either peel the butternut squash or leave the skin on as preferred, then de-seed and cut into big chunks. Place on a lined baking dish, spray with low-calorie cooking spray and sprinkle over the salt, pepper and paprika.

Oven cook the squash at 190°c for 25-30 minutes or until soft. 10 minutes before the squash is done, dice the bacon and scatter into the dish so it cooks with the butternut. Once the time is up, sprinkle over the grated parmesan and place it back in the oven for a minute or two until melted.

Sprinkle the bake with fresh coriander to finish. I like to serve this with couscous cooked in veggie stock.

ROASTED TANDOORI CHICKEN WITH RAITA

5 MINUTES   35 MINUTES   SERVES 4

This dish is all about the quick and easy homemade marinade which packs a real punch. The longer you leave it, the more intense the flavour gets, so marinate overnight for maximum results. Then just whack it in the oven and hey presto, you've got super-tender roasted tandoori chicken.

PER SERVING
226 KCAL
5G CARBS
31G PROTEIN
8G FAT

4 skin-on chicken legs

For the marinade

100g low-fat Greek yoghurt

2 tbsp tandoori masala spice mix

2.5cm fresh ginger, minced

2 cloves of garlic, minced

2 tsp olive oil

Squeeze of lemon juice

Pinch of salt

For the raita

200g fat-free Greek yoghurt

2.5cm cucumber, grated and squeezed

2 tbsp finely chopped fresh coriander

1 tbsp finely chopped fresh mint

½ tsp garam masala

Squeeze of lemon juice

Pinch of salt

For the marinade

Mix all the ingredients together and then rub the marinade into the chicken legs. Leave them in the fridge to marinate for at least 30 minutes or even overnight.

For the raita

Mix all the ingredients together and set aside.

To cook the marinated chicken, place it in a lined ovenproof dish and cover with foil. Cook at 200°c for 30 minutes, remove the foil, then grill for another 5 minutes or until the chicken is cooked and wonderfully charred.

Sprinkle the tandoori chicken with fresh coriander and serve with your homemade raita, basmati rice and salad.

I also like to serve this alongside my flatbreads (see page 192) which I brush with melted butter and minced garlic to turn them into amazing quick garlic naans.

Tips: If you remove the skin from the chicken legs, do this after cooking or the meat will become dry.

MANGO & HONEY
JERK CHICKEN TRAYBAKE

5 MINUTES   15-20 MINUTES   SERVES 4

I love a traybake. If it means less washing up, it's a winner for me. Don't be put off if you can't handle spicy food, as the honey and mango really outweigh the level of spice here.

PER SERVING
443 KCAL
64G CARBS
24G PROTEIN
9G FAT

250g ripe mango, peeled and diced

1 tbsp jerk marinade

1 tbsp honey

2 tsp jerk seasoning

4 chicken thigh fillets

200g long grain rice

400ml boiling water

1 tin of black beans

½ lime

¼ red onion, finely diced

2 tbsp finely diced fresh coriander

Preheat the oven to 200°c. Combine most of the fresh mango, jerk marinade, honey and jerk seasoning in a blender. Place the chicken thighs in an ovenproof dish and add the marinade, massaging in well. Cover with foil and oven cook for 15 minutes.

Remove the chicken from the dish and then pour in the rice and boiling water. Mix well, then drain and rinse the black beans before stirring them in. Place the chicken on top and then put the dish back in the oven, uncovered, for 10-15 minutes or until the rice and chicken are cooked through and all the water has been absorbed.

Finish with a good squeeze of lime juice and then scatter over the red onion, fresh coriander and the remaining mango.

Tips: Fancy this a little more fiery? Add more jerk marinade or a whole red chilli before blending!

CHICKEN & RICE

5 MINUTES   18-20 MINUTES   SERVES 4

Take two very basic ingredients and turn them into something utterly delicious! This quick and easy meal has bags of flavour and there's no fuss required.

PER SERVING
357 KCAL
49G CARBS
21G PROTEIN
9G FAT

4 chicken thigh fillets

1 tbsp chicken seasoning

Salt and pepper

Low-calorie cooking spray

½ onion, finely diced

2 cloves of garlic, minced

400ml hot chicken stock

200g basmati rice, washed

200g frozen mixed veg

Season the chicken thighs with the seasoning and a good pinch of salt and pepper. Spray a large, lidded pan with low-calorie cooking spray and fry the chicken on a medium-high heat for 2 minutes on either side to brown.

Remove the chicken from the pan, then add the onion and garlic. Add more low-calorie spray if needed and fry for 3-4 minutes, adding a tablespoon of water halfway through to soften. Stir in the chicken stock and basmati rice along with a good pinch of pepper. Mix well.

Place the chicken thighs and frozen veg on top of the rice and cook on a low-medium heat for 10-12 minutes or until there is no more liquid in the pan and the rice is cooked. Mix well and enjoy!

Swaps: Can't find chicken seasoning? Swap it for 1 teaspoon of each of these seasonings: paprika, cayenne pepper, onion and garlic granules.

PEPPERONI PIZZA RISOTTO

5 MINUTES   20-25 MINUTES   SERVES 2

This packs in three of your five a day and has all the flavours of a pepperoni pizza…
what more can you ask for?

PER SERVING
425 KCAL
61G CARBS
20G PROTEIN
12G FAT

Low-calorie cooking spray

½ onion, finely diced

7 slices of pepperoni, roughly diced

1 clove of garlic, minced

8 cherry tomatoes, sliced

100g arborio rice

1 tbsp tomato purée

500g passata

1 tsp oregano, plus extra to garnish

Salt and pepper

600ml chicken stock

100g reduced-fat mozzarella

Spray a pan with low-calorie cooking spray, fry the onion and pepperoni on a medium heat for 3-4 minutes until softened, then add the garlic, cherry tomatoes and arborio rice. Mix well and fry for a further 1-2 minutes or until the risotto rice is translucent.

Add the tomato purée, passata, oregano and a pinch of salt and pepper to the pan. Mix well then add a quarter of the stock. Stir again and then wait until the liquid has been absorbed before adding more stock. Repeat until the rice has a slight bite and most of the stock (if not all) has been used, which should take around 20 minutes.

Taste the risotto and adjust the seasoning if needed, then tear the mozzarella into pieces and place them on top. You could also add a few more slices of pepperoni here if you like.

Place the pan under a hot grill for a few minutes to melt the cheese, sprinkle the risotto with oregano and then enjoy!

Tips: Make the risotto creamy by stirring in a dollop of reduced-fat cream cheese!

SPEEDY BIRIYANI

5 MINUTES   25-30 MINUTES   SERVES 4

Layers of chicken coated with beautiful Indian spices, caramelised onions and fluffy fragrant rice will have you coming back for seconds. The best part is that this biriyani is stupidly quick to make and requires minimum effort, as it's all done in one pot.

PER SERVING
421 KCAL
48G CARBS
29G PROTEIN
13G FAT

6 skinless chicken thighs

Low-calorie cooking spray

1 onion, sliced

650g chicken stock

200g long grain rice, washed

2 cloves

1 cinnamon stick

For the marinade

70g fat-free Greek yoghurt

1 tbsp garam masala

½ tsp ground turmeric

1 tsp salt

1 tsp lemon juice

2 cloves of garlic, minced

2.5cm fresh ginger, minced

1 tsp paprika

For the marinade

Combine all the ingredients in a large bowl, then coat the chicken thighs in the marinade. Leave them in the fridge to marinate for at least 30 minutes or even overnight.

Spray a large lidded pan (if you have a cast iron pan, even better) with low-calorie cooking spray and brown the sliced onion on a medium-high heat for 8-10 minutes until dark in colour.

Remove the onion from the pan, add more cooking spray and then fry the marinated chicken for 2 minutes on either side. Take the chicken out and pour in the chicken stock to deglaze the pan, scraping up all the sticky bits. Add the washed rice to the stock, then place the chicken on top and stir in the browned onion, cloves and cinnamon stick.

Put the lid on the pan and simmer for 15-20 minutes, or until the rice is cooked and the water has been absorbed.

Top with a scattering of shop-bought crispy onions for a texture pop. Your biriyani is now ready to serve!

SWEET POTATO, CHICKPEA & SPINACH CURRY

5 MINUTES   25-30 MINUTES   SERVES 2

A super creamy, meat-free coconut curry with an impressive six of your five a day!
This recipe is full of delicious hearty veg and will keep you full for hours.

PER SERVING
466 KCAL
5G CARBS
18G PROTEIN
21G FAT

Low-calorie cooking spray

½ onion, finely diced

2.5cm fresh ginger, minced

2 tbsp curry powder

½ tsp red chilli flakes

1 sweet potato, cubed

1 tin of chickpeas, drained

1 tin of reduced-fat coconut milk

1 tin of chopped tomatoes

½ bag of baby spinach

Salt and pepper

Spray a frying pan with low-calorie cooking spray and fry the onion for 3-4 minutes to soften. Add the ginger, curry powder and chilli flakes to cook for a further minute.

Add the rest of the ingredients except the spinach to the pan, stir well and bring to the boil. Simmer the curry for 20-25 minutes until the sweet potato is lovely and tender.

Stir the spinach into the curry for the last minute of cooking. When done, season to taste with salt and pepper before serving with rice or your preferred accompaniment.

TACO MEATBALLS

 5-10 MINUTES   14-16 MINUTES   SERVES 2

Meatballs with the same flavours as tacos? Yes please. There's even hidden veg in the sauce; no one would ever know they're getting some of their five a day here!

PER SERVING
321 KCAL
18G CARBS
38G PROTEIN
10G FAT

Low-calorie cooking spray

½ red pepper, finely diced

½ onion, finely diced

250g beef mince

12g taco seasoning

500g passata

80g reduced-fat mozzarella, shredded

Spray a pan with low-calorie cooking spray and add the finely diced veg. Fry for 2-3 minutes to soften and then set aside.

Add the beef mince to a bowl with half of the taco seasoning, mix well with your hands and then roll into 8-10 meatballs. Fry in a pan sprayed with low-calorie cooking spray for 6-7 minutes until nicely browned.

Add the passata, cooked veg and the rest of the seasoning to the pan. Mix well and simmer for a further 6-7 minutes. If you like, blend the veg into the passata with a stick blender for a smooth sauce, great for dipping.

Transfer the meatballs and sauce to an ovenproof dish, top with the shredded mozzarella and place under a hot grill for a few minutes to melt the cheese.

Serve this as it comes or with a toasted wrap to dip into the sauce and enjoy!

YIAHNI

Also known as fasolakia yiahni, meaning green beans in tomato sauce, this is one of many Greek dishes my grandparents taught me growing up. It's basically a Greek stew and the trick is to slow-cook it as long as you can so that the lamb is fall-off-the bone tender.

PER SERVING
418 KCAL
22G CARBS
5G PROTEIN
14G FAT

700g lean lamb chops

Low-calorie cooking spray

1 onion, finely diced

1 carrot, finely diced

1 stick of celery, finely diced

1 clove of garlic, minced

½ green chilli, finely diced

2 tomatoes, diced

2 tsp tomato purée

400ml water

1 potato, cubed

200g frozen green beans

Salt and pepper

Spray a large lidded pan with low-calorie cooking spray, brown the lamb chops for a few minutes, then set them aside. In the same pan, fry the onion for 2-3 minutes to soften and then add the carrot, celery, garlic and green chilli.

Stir in about a tablespoon of water to help soften the veg as it cooks for a further few minutes. Add the tomatoes and tomato purée, mix well, then place the lamb chops back into the pan and add the water. Mix again, making sure the lamb chops are submerged as much as possible. Place the lid on, bring to the boil and then simmer for 15 minutes.

After this time, stir the cubed potatoes and green beans into the pan with a little more water if needed. Cook for a further 10-15 minutes, or until the potatoes are soft and the chops are beautifully tender.

Tips: The longer you cook this, the more tender the lamb chops will be!

FAKEAWAYS

CRISPY CHILLI BEEF

 5-10 MINUTES　　 25-30 MINUTES　　⬤ SERVES 2

An all-time takeaway favourite. But why get a takeaway when you can make a fakeaway
for far less calories? It's super easy to make and tastes identical.

PER SERVING
314 KCAL
32G CARBS
31G PROTEIN
7G FAT

1 egg

30g cornflour

250g rump steak

Low-calorie cooking spray

1 clove of garlic, minced

2.5cm fresh ginger, grated

½ red pepper, sliced

½ yellow pepper, sliced

100ml beef stock

½ small red chilli, sliced

1 spring onion, sliced

For the sauce

2 tbsp soy sauce

1 tbsp sweet chilli sauce

1 tbsp tomato ketchup

1 tbsp honey

1 tsp tomato purée

Squeeze of lemon juice

Combine all the ingredients for the sauce in a bowl and set aside. In a separate
bowl, whisk the egg and put the cornflour onto a plate. Slice the steak into
strips, dip into the beaten egg and then coat in the cornflour.

Place the coated steak strips on a lined baking tray and spray with plenty of the
low-calorie cooking spray. Oven cook at 200°c for 20-25 minutes, flipping them
halfway through, until crispy.

Meanwhile, fry the garlic, ginger and sliced peppers in low-calorie cooking
spray for a few minutes, then add the beef stock and the sauce you made
earlier.

Let the mixture simmer for a few minutes until it starts to bubble. Add the crispy
beef, mix well until it's all coated, then serve with boiled rice and garnish with
the sliced chilli and spring onion.

Swaps: Don't fancy beef? Replace with sliced chicken thighs instead. Stay
away from chicken breast though as it'll dry out in this recipe!

SESAME TOFU YAKI UDON

5 MINUTES 10-12 MINUTES SERVES 2

A Japanese stir-fried thick noodle dish ready in under 12 minutes. For the protein, I seasoned tofu with soy sauce and sesame oil for an amazing smoky flavour, but you can use whatever protein you'd like!

PER SERVING
430 KCAL
53G CARBS
20G PROTEIN
14G FAT

125g extra firm tofu, diced

1 tsp soy sauce

1 tsp sesame oil

Low-calorie cooking spray

320g pre-prepared stir-fry vegetables

80g chestnut mushrooms, sliced

300g cooked udon noodles

For the sauce

2 tsp dark soy sauce

1 tsp light soy sauce

2 tbsp oyster sauce

To serve

1 spring onion, finely sliced

A sprinkle of sesame seeds

Coat the tofu in the soy sauce and sesame oil, then fry in a pan on a medium heat for 4-5 minutes until nicely browned. Transfer the tofu to a plate and spray the pan with low-calorie cooking spray.

Add all the vegetables to the pan and fry for 2-3 minutes to soften. Add the udon noodles and fry for a further few minutes.

Turn the temperature up, add the sauce ingredients and mix well for 30 seconds, then mix in the tofu you cooked earlier. Serve straightaway, topped with the spring onion and sesame seeds.

Tips: If you fancy adding more protein to this, scramble an egg or two in the pan when adding the noodles!

SWEET & SOUR PORK

5 MINUTES   18-20 MINUTES   SERVES 2

This dish is all about that thick, sticky sauce and amazing batter you normally get from the Chinese takeaway, but it's full of sugar and fat. I've mimicked the sauce and the batter so you wouldn't believe it's a healthier version.

PER SERVING
447 KCAL
56G CARBS
39G PROTEIN
8G FAT

200g lean pork, diced

2 tsp soy sauce

¼ tsp bicarbonate of soda

1 egg, whisked

20g cornflour

Low-calorie cooking spray

$1/_3$ onion, diced

½ red pepper, diced

½ yellow pepper, diced

2 slices of pineapple, diced

1 clove of garlic, minced

For the sauce

4 tbsp reduced-sugar ketchup

2 tbsp water

1 tbsp soy sauce

1 tsp rice vinegar

1 tsp sweetener

Marinate the diced pork in the soy sauce and bicarbonate of soda for at least 10 minutes. Dip the marinated pork into the whisked egg and then roll in the cornflour until coated. Place on a lined baking tray and coat with low-calorie cooking spray. Oven cook the pork at 180°c for 15-20 minutes or until done, turning and coating with more spray halfway through.

In the meantime, mix the ingredients for the sauce together and set aside. Spray a large frying pan with low-calorie cooking spray and fry the diced veg, pineapple and garlic for 2-3 minutes. Pour in the sauce and crank the heat to high. As soon as it starts to bubble after around 20-30 seconds, add the cooked pork and stir to coat well.

Serve your sweet and sour pork with basmati or egg-fried rice and a sprinkle of sesame seeds on top.

Swaps: Don't fancy pork? Use chicken instead and take out the pineapple if you don't love it like me!

SWEET CHILLI CHICKEN CHOW MEIN

5 MINUTES   20 MINUTES   SERVES 2

Adding batter takes anything from a good dish to a winning one. Add sweet chilli sauce to the mix and life couldn't get any better!

PER SERVING
494 KCAL
65G CARBS
28G PROTEIN
1G FAT

2 chicken thigh fillets, sliced

1 egg, beaten

20g cornflour

Low-calorie cooking spray

300g stir-fry vegetables

2.5cm fresh ginger, minced

1 clove of garlic, minced

125g egg noodles, cooked

1 tbsp dark soy sauce

Chilli flakes, to taste

1 spring onion, sliced

For the sauce

40g reduced-sugar sweet chilli sauce

1 tbsp dark soy sauce

½ tsp rice wine vinegar

½ tsp sweetener

First, make the sauce by combining all the ingredients in a small bowl. Set aside while you prepare the rest of the dish.

Dip the chicken strips into the beaten egg, then the cornflour to coat them completely. Place on a lined baking tray and spray with plenty of low-calorie cooking spray. Oven cook at 180°c for 15-20 minutes, spraying with more cooking spray halfway through.

Spray a pan with low-calorie cooking spray and stir-fry the vegetables, ginger and garlic for 3-4 minutes until slightly softened. Add the cooked noodles and soy sauce to the pan, mix well and then divide between bowls.

Pour the sauce into the now empty pan and crank the heat up high. Once it starts to bubble, add the cooked chicken and stir to coat evenly. Spoon the sweet chilli chicken over the noodle stir-fry, then serve with a sprinkle of dried chilli flakes and the sliced spring onion on top.

Swaps: Substitute the chicken with beef or tofu!

KATSU CURRY RAMEN

5 MINUTES   18-20 MINUTES   SERVES 2

Anyone who is into Japanese food knows that katsu curry is utterly wonderful. I've kept the same flavours of this crowd-pleaser but turned it into a ramen, swapping the rice for noodles and creating a delicious curried broth so you can slurp away.

PER SERVING
496 KCAL
60G CARBS
51G PROTEIN
6G FAT

Low-calorie cooking spray

½ onion, finely diced

½ tsp ground cumin

1 tsp garam masala

1 tbsp curry powder

1 medium carrot, sliced

900ml vegetable stock

1 tsp soy sauce

1 tsp honey

Salt and pepper

2 chicken breasts, tenderised

1 egg, beaten

25g wholemeal or panko breadcrumbs

100g ramen noodles, cooked

Spray a deep saucepan with low-calorie cooking spray and fry the onion for 2-3 minutes until softened. Add the spices and fry for around 30 seconds to release the flavours. Stir in the sliced carrot with a dash of water and cook for a further minute.

Pour the vegetable stock, soy sauce and honey into the pan. Simmer the broth on a medium heat for 10 minutes. Meanwhile, place the tenderised chicken in the beaten egg, then coat in the breadcrumbs. Microwave for 1-2 minutes until lightly softened. Spray the coated chicken with plenty of low-calorie cooking spray and fry for 4 minutes on either side, or until cooked through. You can also cook the chicken in the oven or an air fryer if preferred.

To assemble the ramen, evenly distribute the noodles between 2 bowls, ladle over the broth and place the carrots on one side of the bowls. Slice the chicken and place on top of the ramen. Serve with diced spring onions, half a boiled egg and nori slices.

5-MINUTE DONER KEBAB SALAD BOX

5 MINUTES   5 MINUTES   SERVES 2

Yes, it takes just 5 minutes to cook your own doner kebab at home and it's to die for. Normally a night out staple, a doner kebab is irresistible but seriously calorific. My version has all the flavours of the original and is easy as pie to make.

PER SERVING
389 KCAL
11G CARBS
43G PROTEIN
20G FAT

350g low-fat lamb mince

1 tsp dried oregano

1 tsp ground cumin

1 tsp paprika

½ tsp onion granules

½ garlic granules

Salt and pepper

Low-calorie cooking spray

3 large servings of iceberg lettuce, sliced

3 tomatoes, sliced

3 slices of onion

Place the mince in a large bowl and add the oregano, cumin, paprika, onion and garlic granules along with a good pinch of salt and pepper. Mix well, using your hands to combine everything.

Transfer the seasoned mince to a lined baking tray and place another piece of parchment paper on top. Using a rolling pin, roll out the mince as thinly as possible.

Remove the top piece of parchment paper then spray the flattened mince with low-calorie cooking spray. Grill for 4-5 minutes until cooked through.

Slice the cooked lamb into strips and place the 'doner meat' on top of the salad in a takeaway box. Serve with a few pickled green chillies on top.

Tips: I love serving this with a drizzle of mint sauce mixed with yoghurt!

KING PRAWN PAD THAI

 5 MINUTES   10 MINUTES   SERVES 2

This is one of my favourite dishes from a Thai restaurant, a real classic. Now you can make it in the comfort of your own home.

PER SERVING
398 KCAL
47G CARBS
31G PROTEIN
10G FAT

Low-calorie cooking spray

½ red pepper, sliced

½ yellow pepper, sliced

180g raw king prawns

2 cloves of garlic, minced

2 eggs

100g folded rice noodles, cooked

1 small red chilli, diced

1 spring onion, diced

13g peanuts, chopped

½ lime, cut into wedges

For the sauce

2 tbsp soy sauce

1 tsp light brown sugar

1 tsp sweetener

½ tsp fish sauce

½ tsp white rice vinegar

½ lime, juiced

Mix all the ingredients for the sauce together and then set aside.

Spray a large pan with low-calorie cooking spray and fry the sliced peppers on a medium heat for 2-3 minutes to soften.

Add the king prawns and garlic to the pan and fry for 4-5 minutes, or until the prawns are cooked. Move the ingredients to one side of the pan, crack in the eggs and scramble for 1-2 minutes until cooked.

Quickly stir in the cooked noodles and your sauce. Stir well and divide between bowls, then top with the chilli, spring onion and peanuts. Serve with wedges of lime on the side for squeezing over.

SALT & PEPPER CHICKEN & CHIPS

5-10 MINUTES   20 MINUTES   SERVES 2

Every time I post this recipe on social media, people ask whether I actually made it as it looks like it came straight from your local takeaway. As a bonus, this meal contains a whopping three out of your five a day.

PER SERVING
463 KCAL
34G CARBS
31G PROTEIN
14G FAT

3 chicken thigh fillets, diced

1 egg, beaten

20g cornflour

Low-calorie cooking spray

½ onion, finely diced

1 red pepper, finely diced

1 green pepper, finely diced

½ yellow pepper, finely diced

1 tsp sweetener

1 tsp soy sauce

½ tsp Chinese five spice

Salt and pepper

200g homemade chips

1 spring onion, sliced

Coat the diced chicken in the beaten egg, then in the cornflour. Spray a pan with low-calorie cooking spray and then cook the chicken for 6-7 minutes. Remove from the pan and set aside.

Using the same pan, fry the onion for 2-3 minutes until softened and then add the peppers. Fry for a further few minutes, then stir in the sweetener, soy sauce, five spice and a generous pinch of salt and pepper.

Return the chicken to the pan along with your homemade chips, making sure everything is well coated. Serve your salt and pepper chicken and chips garnished with the sliced spring onion.

Swaps: This also works amazingly with tofu or king prawns!

CHICKEN & HALLOUMI SOUVLAKI

5 MINUTES   7-8 MINUTES   SERVES 2

My Bapou (grandad in Greek) makes the best souvlaki and yes, I know, I'm completely biased. He would sit on the tiniest stool in front of his barbecue watching the skewers turn from the homemade rotisserie feature he added on. Traditionally souvlaki is cooked over an open fire, but this time we're using a griddle pan or grill instead.

PER SERVING
345 KCAL
5G CARBS
56G PROTEIN
12G FAT

2 chicken breasts, diced

50g light halloumi, sliced

Low-calorie cooking spray

2.5cm cucumber, sliced

A handful of lettuce leaves

A handful of cherry tomatoes, halved

For the marinade

100g yoghurt

2 tsp dried oregano

1 clove of garlic, minced

2 tsp extra virgin olive oil

Squeeze of lemon juice

Salt and pepper

For the marinade

Combine all the ingredients in a large bowl and then coat the diced chicken in the marinade. Leave in the fridge to marinate for 30 minutes or even overnight.

Slide the marinated chicken onto skewers soaked in water, followed by the halloumi pieces. Spray with low-calorie cooking spray and then cook in a griddle pan or under the grill on a medium heat for 7-8 minutes, or until the chicken is cooked through.

Serve the souvlaki skewers with your homemade salad and pitta or flatbreads. These are great with a drizzle of homemade tzatziki (see page 200).

TIKKA MASALA ENCHILADAS

5-10 MINUTES   20 MINUTES   SERVES 4

All the flavours of the nation's favourite curry with a Mexican twist. I've added a shortcut by using a ready-made tikka masala paste to amplify the flavours and speed things up.

PER SERVING
403 KCAL
34G CARBS
48G PROTEIN
7G FAT

2 tbsp tikka masala paste

2 cloves of garlic, minced

2.5cm fresh ginger, minced

4 chicken breasts, diced

1 onion, sliced

1 red pepper, sliced

Low-calorie cooking spray

1 tbsp tomato purée

1 tin of chopped tomatoes

90g crème fraiche

Pinch of salt

4 tortilla wraps

50g mozzarella, shredded

Combine half of the tikka masala paste with the minced garlic and ginger, coat the diced chicken in this mixture, then set aside to marinate (the longer the better).

Place a frying pan on a medium heat. Fry the onion and pepper in low-calorie cooking spray for 3-4 minutes until softened. Add the marinated chicken and cook for a further 5 minutes.

Add the remaining tablespoon of tikka masala paste to the pan and cook for a further minute to release the flavours, then stir in the tomato purée and chopped tomatoes. Mix in the crème fraiche and salt, then leave to cool for a few minutes.

Set aside 4 tablespoons of the tikka masala sauce and then divide the chicken mixture between the wraps. Roll up each wrap and lay in an ovenproof dish, seam side down.

Spoon the remaining sauce over the enchiladas and sprinkle the shredded mozzarella on top. Oven cook at 180°c for 14-16 minutes.

Serve the enchiladas with a generous helping of coriander and mint yoghurt on the side.

Tips: You can use chicken thigh fillets instead of breast if you prefer. The tikka masala mixture freezes well so can be made in bigger batches for future meals.

VEGGIE CHILLI NACHOS

 5-10 MINUTES   15 MINUTES   SERVES 3

Homemade paprika-seasoned crispy tortilla chips with a mountain of veggie chilli, melted cheese, guacamole (if you love it like me) and sour cream to dip them straight into. Mexican heaven.

PER SERVING
375 KCAL
49G CARBS
25G PROTEIN
6G FAT

Low-calorie cooking spray

½ onion, finely diced

½ red pepper, finely diced

200g vegetarian mince

2 tsp chilli powder

2 tsp paprika

Salt and pepper

300ml vegetarian stock

1 tin of chopped tomatoes

½ tin of red kidney beans

3 tortilla wraps

1 tsp salt

Spray a large pan with low-calorie cooking spray and then fry the onion and red pepper for 2-3 minutes until softened. Add the vegetarian mince and fry for a few minutes, then stir in the chilli powder, paprika and seasoning to taste.

Mix well and then add the stock, tinned tomatoes and kidney beans to the pan. Bring to the boil and then simmer the chilli for 10-15 minutes or until no liquid remains.

Meanwhile, cut the tortilla wraps into triangles and lay them on a baking tray. Spray with plenty of low-calorie cooking spray and season with a good pinch of salt. Oven cook at 180°c for 5-6 minutes or until your homemade tortilla chips are lovely and crispy.

Serve the chilli in small bowls and place the tortilla chips around the edge. Scoop up and enjoy.

Swaps: Don't fancy using veggie mince? Beef mince would work just as well.

PEPPERONI STUFFED CRUST PIZZA

 10 MINUTES   10-12 MINUTES   SERVES 1

A stuffed crust pizza for under 500 calories and a whopping 37 grams of protein? Hell yes!

PER SERVING
490 KCAL
45G CARBS
37G PROTEIN
8G FAT

50g self-raising flour

75g fat-free Greek yoghurt

Pinch of salt

2 Cheestrings

1 tbsp tomato purée

½ tsp dried oregano

30g cheddar, grated

½ red pepper, sliced

4 cherry tomatoes, sliced

15g pepperoni

Mix the flour, yoghurt and salt together until the mixture forms a dough. Roll out on a floured surface to roughly the thickness of a pound coin.

Cut each Cheestring into 5 pieces. Place the pieces around the edge of the pizza base and fold the dough over them, pushing down to seal it shut. This is your stuffed crust.

Spread the tomato purée evenly over the base, then sprinkle the oregano on top. Add your grated cheese, sliced pepper, cherry tomatoes and pepperoni. Place the pizza on a lined baking tray and oven cook at 200°c for 10-12 minutes. Serve the pizza with a side salad.

Swaps: Use any of your favourite pizza toppings with this base: go wild!

BIG STACK BAGEL

5 MINUTES   4-6 MINUTES   SERVES 2

No need to go to your favourite takeaway when you can make this copy-cat recipe at home!
Instead of your usual burger bun, we're going for a bagel to create the stack of dreams.

PER SERVING
449 KCAL
49G CARBS
39G PROTEIN
12G FAT

250g beef mince

Low-calorie cooking spray

Salt and pepper

2 tbsp low-fat burger sauce

3 thin bagels

80g iceberg lettuce, sliced

4 light cheese singles

3 slices of onion, finely diced

1 gherkin, finely diced

Divide the beef mince into 4 balls and place in a large frying pan sprayed with low-calorie cooking spray. Using a burger press or the back of a spatula and a piece of parchment paper, press down to form a thin patty.

Season the patty with salt and pepper and fry on a medium-high heat for 2-3 minutes remembering to season the other side when flipping.

Spread burger sauce on the bottom halves of 2 bagels, then layer up half of the lettuce, patties and cheese in that order. Grab the spare bagel and place a half on top of each patty. Add more burger sauce to the bagel, then layer up the remaining lettuce, patties and cheese. Scatter over the onions and gherkins, then top each stack with the remaining bagel halves.

Serve with a side of chips for the real fakeaway experience and enjoy!

Tips: Use standard bagels cut into 3 pieces horizontally if you can't find the thin ones.

STREET
FOOD

CHICKEN TINGA TACOS

5 MINUTES   16-18 MINUTES   SERVES 2

You may have heard of birria tacos – slow-cooked beef stew with Mexican chillies – but the chipotle paste in this recipe is much easier to find in the supermarket, and tinga is way quicker too! It's shredded chicken in a smoky chipotle and tomato sauce which makes a delicious taco filling.

PER SERVING
474 KCAL
5G CARBS
37G PROTEIN
10G FAT

For the tinga

Low-calorie cooking spray

2 chicken breasts

1 clove of garlic, minced

350g chicken stock

100g passata

2 tbsp chipotle paste

½ tsp dried oregano

¼ tsp ground cumin

Salt and pepper

For the tacos

4 mini tortilla wraps

75g reduced-fat mozzarella, shredded

For the salsa

2 tomatoes, finely diced

2 slices of onion, finely diced

2 tbsp finely chopped fresh coriander

½ lime, juiced

For the tinga

Spray a large lidded pan with low-calorie cooking spray and fry the chicken breasts on a high heat for 2 minutes either side until browned. For the last minute, add the garlic, then stir in the remaining ingredients including a pinch of salt and pepper and bring to the boil.

Once the sauce is boiling, turn the heat down to a simmer and leave for 10 minutes or until the chicken is cooked. Remove the chicken and shred using two forks.

For the tacos

Dip a tortilla wrap into the tinga sauce, then fry in a large frying pan sprayed with low-calorie cooking spray for 1-2 minutes on a medium heat. Place a portion of shredded chicken on one side of the tortilla, pour over 1-2 tablespoons of tinga sauce and then top with shredded mozzarella.

Fold the tortilla in half to cover the filling and carefully flip. Cook on the other side for a further 1-2 minutes, or until the cheese has melted and the tortilla is crispy. Repeat this whole process with the remaining tortillas, chicken and cheese.

For the salsa

Mix all the ingredients together, then open the tinga tacos and fill them up with the salsa. Pour the remaining tinga sauce into a bowl, dip your tacos in and enjoy!

GYROS

 5 MINUTES 7-8 MINUTES 🔘 SERVES 2

Traditionally, gyros is a Greek dish made from meat cooked on a vertical rotisserie with chips, salad and tzatziki all in a flatbread. If you're like me and don't have a rotisserie lying around, grilling the chicken works just as well and makes it just as tender, in a quarter of the time.

PER SERVING
417 KCAL
47G CARBS
30G PROTEIN
12G FAT

2 chicken thighs, diced

Low-calorie cooking spray

1 tomato, sliced

2 slices of red onion

100g homemade chips

Pinch of paprika

2 x 2-ingredient flatbreads
(see page 192)

For the marinade

3 tbsp yoghurt

1 clove of garlic, minced

2 tsp paprika

1 tsp dried oregano

½ tsp ground cumin

½ tsp ground coriander

Salt and pepper

Squeeze of lemon juice

First, combine all the ingredients for the marinade in a shallow bowl, coat the diced chicken in the mixture and then leave to marinate for 30 minutes or even overnight.

Grill the marinated chicken in a pan sprayed with low-calorie cooking spray for 7-8 minutes or until cooked through, then slice up.

To assemble the gyros, divide the salad, chicken and chips between the flatbreads. Finish with a sprinkle of paprika and then serve with tzatziki (see my recipe on page 200).

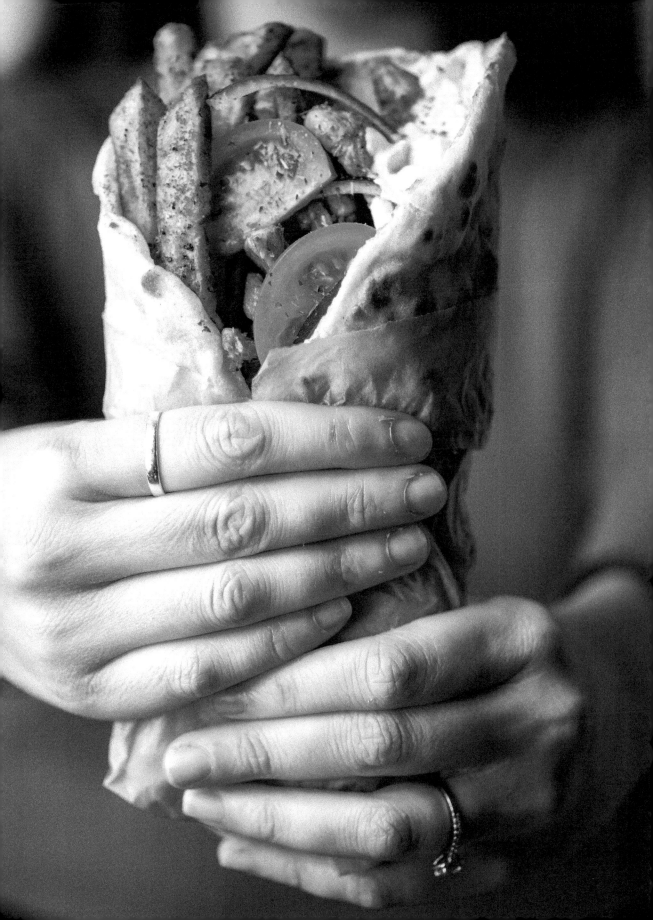

BEEF BULGOGI

 5 MINUTES   7-8 MINUTES   SERVES 2

Marinated slices of beef are grilled to perfection in this Korean staple, also known as 'fire meat' because the meat is normally cooked on a barbecue or grilled. It's generally served with rice but I decided on a low-carb lettuce wrap to get stuck into.

PER SERVING
253 KCAL
19G CARBS
28G PROTEIN
9G FAT

Low-calorie cooking spray

½ onion, sliced

½ yellow pepper, sliced

1 lean ribeye steak at room temperature

Salt and pepper

4 iceberg lettuce leaves

1 spring onion, diced

For the sauce

2.5cm fresh ginger, minced

1 clove of garlic, minced

1 tbsp light soy sauce

2 tsp dark soy sauce

2 tsp honey

1 tsp sesame oil

In a bowl, mix all the ingredients for the sauce together and set aside. Spray a large frying pan with low-calorie cooking spray and fry the sliced onion and pepper for a few minutes to soften. Remove the veg from the pan and set aside.

Spray the steak with plenty of low-calorie cooking spray and season well with salt and pepper on both sides. Fry the steak in the same pan on a high heat for 2 minutes on either side. Let it rest for 4 minutes on a chopping board, then slice into strips at an angle.

Pour the sauce into the hot pan and when it starts to bubble, place the pieces of steak back in and stir to coat well. Apportion the veg between the lettuce leaves, place the steak on top, sprinkle with diced spring onion and enjoy.

Swaps: Any steak will work here, as would beef mince or even chicken strips!

BLACK BEAN CHIMICHANGA WITH LIME AND CORIANDER RICE

5 MINUTES   18-20 MINUTES   SERVES 3

Filled with chipotle seasoned veg, there is no need for a deep-fat fryer when you can pan-fry these chimichangas to release the most amazing, toasted flavours. The real icing on the cake is that they're topped with melted cheese!

PER SERVING
451 KCAL
72G CARBS
20G PROTEIN
7G FAT

Low-calorie cooking spray

½ onion, finely diced

½ red and yellow pepper, finely diced

1 tin of black beans, drained and rinsed

1 tin of chopped tomatoes

½ mug of boiling water

40g chipotle paste

Salt and pepper

½ lime, juiced

2-3 tbsp finely chopped fresh coriander

120g basmati rice, cooked

3x tortilla wraps

50g light cheddar, grated

In a large pan with some low-calorie cooking spray, fry the onion on a low-medium heat for 2-3 minutes to soften. Add the peppers and fry for a further few minutes, then stir in the black beans, tinned tomatoes, boiling water and chipotle paste. Stir well, season with salt and pepper to taste, then simmer for 10 minutes or until the veg has softened and all the liquid has been absorbed.

Meanwhile, stir the lime juice and fresh coriander into the cooked rice and season to taste. Lay out the tortillas one at a time on a chopping board, spoon a portion of rice into the centre, then a portion of the black bean filling on top. Fold the sides of the tortilla in towards the middle then roll up like a burrito and repeat.

Spray a large ovenproof saucepan with low-calorie cooking spray and place each chimichanga seam-side down. Fry on all sides for a few minutes until the tortillas are lovely and brown.

Scatter the grated cheese over each chimichanga and place under a hot grill until melted. Serve them as is or with a salad on the side.

CURRIED PORK STEAKS WITH MINTED CUCUMBER SALAD

10 MINUTES   8-10 MINUTES   SERVES 2

What a flavour sensation this is! I find that pork can be very dry, so I made a beautiful marinade to lock in the juices, paired with a fresh minted cucumber salad to give it extra zing.

PER SERVING
419 KCAL
9G CARBS
40G PROTEIN
25G FAT

3 pork steaks or chops, fat trimmed off

2 tsp olive oil

1 tbsp curry powder

1 tsp paprika

½ tsp ground turmeric

2.5cm fresh ginger, minced

2 sprigs of coriander

1 clove of garlic, minced

½ chilli, finely diced

Salt and pepper

Squeeze of lemon juice

Low-calorie cooking spray

For the cucumber salad

160g iceberg lettuce, finely diced

5cm cucumber, finely diced

½ red onion, finely diced

1 large sprig of mint, finely chopped

Squeeze of lemon juice

Using your hands, massage the pork steaks or chops with the olive oil, then add the remaining ingredients except the cooking spray and massage until coated. Marinate the pork for at least 10 minutes (the longer the better).

Spray a griddle pan with low-calorie cooking spray and fry the marinated pork on a medium-high heat for 4 minutes on either side. Remove and let them rest.

For the cucumber salad

While the pork is resting, prepare the salad. Simply mix all the ingredients together in a bowl.

Serve the curried pork with the salad and a good dollop of fat-free Greek yoghurt.

Tips: Use a frying pan if you don't have a griddle. Cooking the steaks or chops under the grill works too!

HOISIN 'DUCK' LOADED FRIES

5-10 MINUTES   20-25 MINUTES   SERVES 2

A fun change from your usual duck pancakes which are seriously addictive. This may sound crazy but I'm using crispy mushrooms to imitate the duck! Loaded onto homemade fries, topped with spring onions and cucumber, finished with a drizzle of that beautifully rich hoisin sauce: I know you want to dig right in.

PER SERVING
277 KCAL
59G CARBS
7G PROTEIN
2G FAT

2 potatoes, cut into chips

2 tsp Chinese five spice

Salt and pepper

Low-calorie cooking spray

200g chestnut mushrooms, thinly sliced

18g cornflour

2 tbsp hoisin sauce

2 spring onions, thinly sliced

7-8cm cucumber, thinly sliced

Place the potato in a large bowl, season with 1 teaspoon of the five spice and a good pinch of salt and pepper, then spread the chips out on a lined baking tray. Spray generously with low-calorie cooking spray and oven cook at 180°c for 20-25 minutes, turning the chips and spraying again halfway through.

Meanwhile, coat the sliced mushrooms in the cornflour and remaining five spice. Place on a lined baking tray and spray with plenty of low-calorie cooking spray. Oven cook at 200°c for 8-10 minutes or until crispy, then toss them in the hoisin sauce.

To assemble, place the chips onto a serving dish, followed by the spring onions and cucumber, then the hoisin mushrooms. For an extra pop of flavour, drizzle over more of that delicious hoisin sauce just before serving.

Swaps: Oyster mushrooms work amazingly well for this dish. If you can find them (as they can be hard to track down!) tear them into strips rather than slicing. But if you really don't fancy using mushrooms, use vegetarian duck instead.

LAMB KARAHI

5-10 MINUTES   25-30 MINUTES   SERVES 2

A Pakistani curry with tender pieces of lamb in a rich and delicious tomato-based gravy. Please don't be put off by the long list of ingredients, as you'll probably have most of them at home already. This goes perfectly with my fragrant rice recipe on page 186.

PER SERVING
424 KCAL
23G CARBS
59G PROTEIN
11G FAT

Low-calorie cooking spray

½ onion, sliced

300g lean lamb, diced

1 tin of chopped tomatoes

1 tbsp tomato purée

2.5cm fresh ginger, minced

3 cloves of garlic, minced

1 green chilli, finely diced

2 tsp garam masala

1 tsp paprika

1 tsp ground coriander

½ tsp ground cumin

½ tsp chilli powder

¼ tsp ground turmeric

350ml water

2 tbsp yoghurt

Salt and pepper

1 tsp lemon juice

2 tbsp roughly chopped fresh coriander

Spray a large lidded pan with plenty of low-calorie cooking spray and fry the onion on a medium heat for 3-4 minutes until softened. Add the diced lamb and fry for a further few minutes to brown, then add the tomatoes, purée, ginger, garlic, green chilli and all the spices with a splash of water. Mix well and cook for around 1 minute.

Add the water, yoghurt and a good pinch of salt and pepper, then simmer the mixture for at least 15-20 minutes, but the longer the better. Add a bit more water if you're cooking it for a lot longer.

Cook the curry until the sauce has thickened and the lamb is lovely and tender. Finish with the lemon juice and fresh coriander, then serve with the fragrant rice and enjoy!

Swaps: Swap the lamb for bone-in skinless chicken pieces and add another fresh chilli for more of a kick!

CHUNKY FAJITA TAQUITOS

5 MINUTES 10-15 MINUTES SERVES 2

A taquito is basically a thin rolled taco, traditionally shallow fried to get a crispy exterior with toppings like sour cream and guacamole. With my version, you still get a crispy exterior from lightly frying them and a chunky taquito that's bursting with fajita seasoned veg and super tender charred steak strips.

PER SERVING
376 KCAL
36G CARBS
34G PROTEIN
9G FAT

1 rump steak, at room temperature

1 tsp olive oil

Salt and pepper

Low-calorie cooking spray

½ onion, sliced

½ red pepper, sliced

½ green pepper, sliced

½ yellow pepper, sliced

20g fajita seasoning

1 tbsp tomato purée

2 tbsp water

4 tortilla wraps

Rub the steak evenly with the olive oil, then season well with a good pinch of salt and pepper. Fry in a very hot, dry pan (it needs to sizzle as soon as the steak touches it) for 2 minutes on either side over a high heat. If you have an extractor fan, stick it on for this. Remove the steak and let it rest.

Spray the same pan with low-calorie cooking spray and fry the onion for 2-3 minutes to soften. Add the sliced peppers and fry for a few minutes on a medium heat to soften. Add the fajita seasoning, tomato purée and water. Mix well and fry for a further 1-2 minutes until the veg becomes lovely and sticky.

Once the steak has rested, slice at an angle into thin strips. Next, grab a wrap and add a quarter of the seasoned veg in a line down the middle. Place a few strips of beef on top and wrap up, then slice in half and place seam-side down in a clean frying pan sprayed with low-calorie cooking spray.

Repeat until you have 4 taquitos and then fry them in the pan for a few minutes to brown on all sides. Spray with more low-calorie cooking spray for extra crispiness.

Tips: Top the taquitos with whatever you like; this could be salad, melted cheese or sour cream and salsa!

OKONOMIYAKI

 5 MINUTES   8 MINUTES   SERVES 2

A delicious Japanese savoury pancake made up of batter and veg including diced cabbage,
topped with bacon pieces and a beautiful array of Japanese sauces to take it to the next level.
This street food dish is perfect for using up any remaining veg in your fridge.

PER SERVING
327 KCAL
38G CARBS
24G PROTEIN
8G FAT

2 eggs

70g plain flour

½ tsp baking powder

100ml cold water

1 tsp soy sauce

200g cabbage, finely diced

100g chestnut mushrooms, diced

Low-calorie cooking spray

For the toppings

4 cooked bacon medallions, diced

2 spring onions, diced

2 tbsp light mayonnaise

1 tbsp teriyaki sauce

1 tbsp soy sauce

In a large bowl, whisk the eggs, flour, baking powder, water and soy sauce together well, then fold in the diced cabbage and mushrooms. Spray a small pan generously with low-calorie cooking spray and then when it's hot, add the batter.

Using a spatula, make sure the pancake is compact by pushing the mixture away from the edges into the middle of the pan. After around 4 minutes, grab a large plate, place it on top of the pan and carefully flip so you can slide the pancake back into the pan with the cooked side facing up.

Fry the pancake for a further 4 minutes or until cooked through, then transfer to a plate. Add all the toppings and enjoy.

Tips: Kewpie mayonnaise (Japanese mayo) goes amazingly well with this dish!

PANKO AUBERGINE & SOY MUSHROOM BAO BUNS

5 MINUTES   3-6 MINUTES   SERVES 6

Bao buns are soft, fluffy, warm pillows of steamed dough ready to be filled and devoured.
To contrast with the texture of the buns, my favourite filling is crunchy panko aubergine and
soy-glazed shiitake mushrooms, but you go wild and get creative.

PER SERVING
110 KCAL
21G CARBS
3G PROTEIN
1G FAT

6 slices of aubergine

Pinch of salt

Low-calorie cooking spray

30ml oat milk

20g plain flour

20g panko breadcrumbs

1 pack of shiitake mushrooms, sliced

2 tsp soy sauce

6 ready-made bao buns

1-2 sprigs of fresh coriander

2 radishes, sliced

2 tbsp light mayo

Sriracha, to taste (optional)

Season the aubergine with salt, then spray a frying pan with low-calorie cooking spray and fry the slices for a few minutes to soften. In a bowl, mix the oat milk and flour together to make a batter. Dip the cooked aubergine slices into the batter and then into the panko breadcrumbs until coated.

Spray the battered aubergine generously with low-calorie cooking spray and fry for a few minutes. In a small saucepan, cook the mushrooms with the soy sauce for a few minutes until they become lovely and soft.

Assemble the cooked veg evenly in the bao buns, then add a few fresh coriander leaves and radish slices to each. Drizzle over the mayonnaise and add sriracha if you want a kick. Enjoy!

TURKISH PIDE

5 MINUTES   22-24 MINUTES   SERVES 2

An oval-shaped flatbread resembling a boat with crispy sides and various combinations of toppings, Turkish pide is a lovely change from your standard pizza fakeaway.

PER SERVING
356 KCAL
35G CARBS
36G PROTEIN
8G FAT

½ onion, finely diced

Low-calorie cooking spray

200g beef mince

2 tbsp tomato purée

2 tbsp water

½ tsp ground cumin

½ tsp paprika

½ tsp dried thyme

Salt and pepper

2 cooked flatbreads (see page 192)

Black sesame seeds (optional)

For the toppings

30g reduced-fat mozzarella, shredded or grated

4 cherry tomatoes, sliced

OR

¼ red pepper, finely diced

¼ green pepper, finely diced

In a large pan, fry the onion in low-calorie cooking spray for 2-3 minutes to soften, then add the beef mince and fry for 4-5 minutes or until cooked. Stir in the tomato purée and water, then season with the cumin, paprika, thyme, salt and pepper.

Place the flatbreads on a lined baking tray or pizza tray, then spoon the mince into the centre of each one, avoiding the edges. Pinch both ends of the flatbread together to seal and then fold the sides in to form a boat-shape (Google this if you get stuck!). If you like, sprinkle the crusts with black sesame seeds.

For the toppings

Cover the mince with either mozzarella and cherry tomatoes or diced red and green pepper. Now oven bake the pide at 200°c for 14-16 minutes, or until beautifully golden on top.

Tips: Invest in metal or mesh pizza trays; they make any dough recipe turn out brilliantly!

VIETNAMESE SPRING ROLLS WITH SATAY DIP

 5-10 MINUTES   SERVES 2

Beautiful rice paper rolls with a huge flavour punch! These are filled with fragrant herbs
and a rainbow of veg, ready to be dipped into a luscious satay sauce.
The perfect combo of delectable goodness.

PER SERVING
362 KCAL
56G CARBS
33G PROTEIN
11G FAT

6 rice paper wrappers

18 king prawns, cooked

2.5cm cucumber, cut into thin strips

1 small carrot, cut into thin strips

Fresh mint leaves, to taste

3 sprigs of coriander, halved

1 little gem lettuce

For the satay dip

20g peanut butter

1 tsp soy sauce

1 tsp sweetener

2-3 tbsp water

For the satay dip

In a small bowl, mix all the ingredients together, using the remaining tablespoon of water to adjust the sauce to your desired thickness. Set aside.

Fill a wide bowl with hot water and, working with one at a time, submerge the rice paper wrappers in the water for a few seconds, then remove and place onto a chopping board.

Working quickly, place 3 prawns in a line down the centre of the wrapper, followed by the vegetables, 1 or 2 mint leaves, half a sprig of coriander and a lettuce leaf.

Working from the bottom, roll the rice paper over the filling, then fold the left and right edges of the rice paper into the centre. Firmly roll up to make your beautiful rice paper roll. I promise you, if you're struggling with this now you will 100% get better the more you practice!

Repeat until you have used up all the rice paper wrappers and filling, then serve the rolls with your satay dipping sauce and enjoy.

Tips: Mix and match the herbs and vegetables to make these rice paper rolls your perfect bite!

SIDES & SNACKS

BANG BANG CAULIFLOWER

5 MINUTES   20-25 MINUTES   SERVES 2

Lightly battered cauliflower florets give this irresistible snack a lovely texture,
especially when coated in the sticky sauce. I've made the heat mild but add more sriracha
if you like it hot, hot, hot.

PER SERVING
156 KCAL
34G CARBS
4G PROTEIN
1G FAT

300g cauliflower florets

Low-calorie cooking spray

35g cornflour

Salt and pepper

For the sauce

2 tbsp reduced-fat sweet chilli sauce

1 tbsp honey

2 tsp sriracha

1 tsp soy sauce

Squeeze of lemon juice

In a large bowl, spray the cauliflower florets with low-calorie cooking spray and then dust with the cornflour until nicely coated. Transfer to a lined baking dish and spray with more cooking spray, then oven cook at 200°c for 20-25 minutes or until softened.

In a small bowl, mix all the ingredients for the sauce together. Wipe the large bowl clean, then place the cooked cauliflower back in and pour over the sauce. Mix until evenly coated, serve and enjoy.

Tips: Add half a teaspoon each of garlic powder and paprika to the cornflour for extra flavour!

HALLOUMI FRIES

5 MINUTES · 12-14 MINUTES · SERVES 2

What Greek doesn't like halloumi? I use it in so many recipes and never get bored.
These halloumi fries are crispy on the outside and melt-in-your-mouth on the inside using
my two-part cooking method. With no deep fat fryer in sight, eating these won't play havoc
with your waistline.

PER SERVING
229 KCAL
10G CARBS
18G PROTEIN
13G FAT

140g light halloumi

15g cornflour

½ tsp mixed herbs

½ tsp garlic powder

Pinch of black pepper

Low-calorie cooking spray

Slice the halloumi into thick chip shapes. In a bowl, mix the cornflour with the herbs, garlic and black pepper before dipping the halloumi into the seasoned coating.

Spray a frying pan with low-calorie cooking spray and fry the halloumi on a medium heat for 2-3 minutes to crispen on all sides.

Spray the fries with more low-calorie cooking spray and place in an air-fryer or oven at 180°c for 8-10 minutes to get them extra crispy.

Top the halloumi fries with your favourite sauces and sprinkle on some dried parsley if you like. Enjoy!

Tips: Mix peri-peri sauce with light mayonnaise for a beautiful, creamy dipping sauce to serve alongside your halloumi fries.

CROWD-PLEASING RICE SENSATIONS

5-10 MINUTES   10 MINUTES   SERVES 2

These two rice dishes pair perfectly with a lot of different cuisines and countless recipes in this book. The fragrant rice goes especially well with a curry and the egg fried rice is perfect with any Chinese dish. You could also add some protein (like chicken, tofu, pork or prawns) and eat the fried rice as a lip-smackingly good main meal.

PER SERVING
EGG FRIED
267 KCAL
42G CARBS
11G PROTEIN
6G FAT
FRAGRANT
182 KCAL
42G CARBS
4G PROTEIN
1G FAT

Egg Fried Rice

2 eggs

Salt and pepper

2 spring onions, sliced

Low-calorie cooking spray

150g frozen mixed veg

200g cold cooked white rice

1 tbsp teriyaki sauce

1 tbsp soy sauce

1 tsp sweetener

Fragrant Rice

100g basmati rice

200ml cold water

1 whole clove

1 star anise segment

¼ tsp ground turmeric

Egg Fried Rice

Crack the eggs into a bowl, season with a pinch of salt and pepper, whisk and then add the spring onions. Spray a large frying pan with low-calorie cooking spray, then wait until it's hot before adding the eggs. Leave to cook for around 10-15 seconds, then scramble.

Add the frozen mixed veg to the pan and fry for 2 minutes, then add the rice and remaining ingredients to season. Fry for a further 2-3 minutes or until the veg has heated through.

Fragrant Rice

Place the rice in a lidded pan, cover with the cold water, then add the rest of the ingredients. As soon as it starts to boil, cover with the lid and reduce the heat to a simmer. Cook the rice for 10 minutes, remove the clove and star anise, mix well and serve.

BRUSCHETTA

I literally can't stop shovelling these once I've made a batch. They are moreish bites that make me and any guests that come round go wild for more.

PER SERVING
82 KCAL
13G CARBS
1G PROTEIN
2G FAT

1 punnet of cherry or plum tomatoes, diced

2 slices of red onion, finely diced

1 tbsp extra virgin olive oil

Squeeze of lemon juice

1 clove of garlic, peeled and halved

6 gluten-free ciabatta rolls, sliced and toasted

4-5 basil leaves

2 tbsp balsamic glaze

Mix the diced tomatoes with the onion, olive oil and lemon juice in a bowl. Rub the cut side of the garlic clove over the toasted ciabatta slices then divide the topping evenly between them. Roughly tear the basil leaves over the top and add a drizzle of balsamic glaze to finish.

Tips: Add an extra drizzle of olive oil at the end... it's totally worth it!

CHEESY GARLIC TEAR & SHARE

5-10 MINUTES   14-16 MINUTES   SERVES 9-10

Tear and shares are just a thing of beauty but it's so tempting to eat the whole lot yourself! This recipe uses the magical 2-ingredient dough which is made in minutes, with oozing mozzarella in each dough ball, all glazed with buttery garlic and herbs. Brilliant for a dinner party or to wow the family.

PER SERVING
68 KCAL
8G CARBS
4G PROTEIN
2G FAT

100g self-raising flour

160g fat-free thick Greek yoghurt

Pinch of salt

100g mozzarella or Cheestrings

1 tbsp light butter, melted

1 clove of garlic, minced

½ tsp finely chopped fresh parsley

In a large bowl, mix the flour, yoghurt and salt together to form a dough. Turn out on a floured surface, divide the dough into 9 or 10 equal balls, then stuff each ball with a cube of mozzarella or Cheestring and roll back into an even sphere.

Place the stuffed dough balls into a lined round ovenproof dish. Mix the melted butter with the minced garlic and fresh parsley, then brush half of this mixture over the dough balls.

Oven cook at 180°c for 14-16 minutes or until the dough balls are cooked through, then brush over the remaining garlic butter while still hot and enjoy.

Tips: Add pieces of pepperoni to the dough balls with the cheese for a meaty surprise!

2-INGREDIENT FLATBREADS

🕐 5 MINUTES 🍳 5 MINUTES 🍽 SERVES 2

I haven't used shop-bought flatbreads since I created this recipe. All hail the miracle that is this no-knead, no-proof, no-rest dough! Made in minutes, you can use it for other bread like naans or pizza bases... the options are endless. I've been obsessed with this dough for years and I've got a feeling you will be too.

PER SERVING
159 KCAL
28G CARBS
8G PROTEIN
1G FAT

80g self-raising flour

80g fat-free thick Greek yoghurt

Mix the flour and yoghurt together with a pinch of salt until the mixture forms a ball. Transfer the dough to a floured surface and divide into 2 equal parts. Roll out each piece to a flatbread shape around 8-10cm long using a floured rolling pin.

In a griddle or frying pan, dry-fry each flatbread on a medium-high heat for 1-2 minutes each side until cooked. If you like, brush with melted butter and garlic powder to make a beautiful garlic naan!

Swaps: You can use natural instead of Greek yoghurt but adjust the measurements if so as you won't need as much.

SPANAKOPITA FILO TRIANGLES

10-15 MINUTES   14-16 MINUTES   SERVES 14

I promise the prep is totally worthwhile for these heavenly little parcels of spinach, feta and ricotta wrapped in crisp filo pastry. The moment you bite into them, you'll be transported to the Mediterranean.

PER SERVING
116 KCAL
13G CARBS
6G PROTEIN
5G FAT

250g spinach, blanched

Low-calorie cooking spray

1 onion, finely diced

2 cloves of garlic, minced

3 tbsp finely chopped fresh parsley

1-2 tsp finely chopped fresh chives

1-2 tsp finely chopped fresh mint

1 tsp grated nutmeg

Salt and pepper

1 egg

100g ricotta

180g feta, crumbled

270g filo pastry sheets

Remove any excess water from the blanched spinach, roughly chop and set aside. Spray a large pan with low-calorie cooking spray, then cook the onion, garlic and herbs for 4-5 minutes until softened. Stir in the chopped spinach and nutmeg, then season with salt and pepper to taste.

In a large bowl, mix the egg, ricotta and crumbled feta together. Add the spinach mixture to the bowl, stirring well to make your filling.

Slice 7 sheets of the filo pastry in half widthways to make 14 pieces. Grabbing a sheet at a time and keeping the rest under a damp kitchen towel to stop them from drying out, spray one side of the pastry with low-calorie cooking spray and fold in half so the dry side faces outwards, pressing gently to stick the layers down.

Spray the folded pastry again with low-calorie cooking spray and then place a heaped tablespoon of the filling in the centre. Fold the pastry diagonally over the mixture so it forms a small triangle and repeat on the other side to make a parcel.

Continue assembling the spanakopita with the remaining pastry until the filling is used up, making sure you use more low-calorie cooking spray to fold away any remaining pastry.

Place the parcels on a lined baking tray and spray with low-calorie cooking spray. Oven cook for 15 minutes at 180°c or until golden and enjoy.

Tips: These are great for freezing and there's no need to cook them before you do!

CARAMELISED ONION AND CHEDDAR SAUSAGE ROLLS

5-10 MINUTES 14-16 MINUTES SERVES 16

These vegetarian sausages are super moreish; you'll need a lot of willpower to stop yourself eating half the batch! The caramelised onion chutney adds a hint of sweetness but if you prefer to make the filling plain, they are just as scrumptious.

PER SERVING
77 KCAL
6G CARBS
3G PROTEIN
4G FAT

190g ready-rolled puff pastry

4 meat-free sausages, de-skinned

2 tbsp caramelised red onion chutney

50 light cheddar cheese, grated

1 egg, beaten

Black sesame seeds (optional)

Keep the pastry on the parchment paper it comes with and slice in half lengthways, saving one half for another recipe. Place the sausage meat evenly in the middle of the pastry and then use a teaspoon to spread the caramelised onion chutney over the sausage meat. Sprinkle the grated cheddar evenly over the top.

Fold the pastry over the filling so the edges meet, then use a fork to crimp the pastry together and enclose the filling. Cut the roll into 16 pieces and carefully place them on a lined baking tray with enough room to expand.

Brush each sausage roll with the beaten egg and if you want, add a sprinkle of black sesame seeds on the tops. Oven cook at 180°c for 14-16 minutes or until the sausage is cooked through.

Tips: To make these vegan, simply buy vegan puff pastry and brush with plant-based milk instead of egg!

IRRESISTIBLE SCOTCH EGGS

5-10 MINUTES   20 MINUTES   SERVES 4

Scotch eggs are normally deep fried but to save on calories, we're baking them instead. They become lovely and crispy with the help of low-calorie cooking spray and the sausage meat stays succulent inside.

PER SERVING
223 KCAL
14G CARBS
23G PROTEIN
8G FAT

6 reduced-fat sausages, de-skinned

2 tsp dried parsley

Salt and pepper

4 eggs, hard-boiled

1 egg, whisked

40g panko breadcrumbs

Low-calorie cooking spray

Put the sausage meat into a bowl, add the parsley and season with a good pinch of salt and pepper. Divide the mixture into 4 equal balls and then, using wet hands and working with one at a time, flatten them out to an even thickness between your palms.

Gently wrap the sausage meat patties around the peeled hard-boiled eggs, enclosing them completely and shaping into a ball. Dip each ball into the whisked egg and then roll gently in the panko breadcrumbs, fully coating each one.

Place the scotch eggs on a lined baking tray and spray with plenty of low-calorie cooking spray. Oven bake them at 180°c for 15 minutes, then turn the temperature up to 220°c for a further 5 minutes, or until the sausage meat is cooked and the scotch eggs have browned nicely.

Swaps: Make these veggie by using vegetarian sausages, and try using wholemeal breadcrumbs instead.

MY CHAMPION DIPS

5-10 MINUTES   10 MINUTES   SERVES 4

These are my ultimate two dips. They're a great accompaniment for so many dishes but also great to have on their own with a side of warm pitta for dipping.

PER SERVING
TZATZIKI
55 KCAL
3G CARBS
6G PROTEIN
3G FAT

RED PEPPER
35 KCAL
1G CARBS
1G PROTEIN
1G FAT

Tzatziki

200g cucumber, grated

200g fat-free Greek yoghurt

1 clove of garlic, minced

2 tsp finely diced fresh mint

2 tsp extra virgin olive oil

Squeeze of lemon juice

Pinch of salt

Red Pepper

3 red peppers, halved

3 large tomatoes, halved

Low-calorie cooking spray

½ tsp salt

Tzatziki

Using your hands, squeeze the grated cucumber over the sink to remove as much liquid as possible, then put the cucumber in a bowl. Mix in the rest of the ingredients and adjust the seasoning to suit.

Red Pepper

Remove the stems and seeds from the red peppers and place them cut side down on a lined baking tray along with the halved tomatoes. Spray with low-calorie cooking spray and grill on high for 10 minutes. Remove the skin from the tomatoes, then blend the peppers and tomatoes together with the salt. Adjust the seasoning to taste.

EASY-PEASY GYOZAS

10-15 MINUTES   3-4 MINUTES   SERVES 35

I am a real sucker for gyozas and would happily eat a plateful on their own. They are surprisingly easily to make but you do need a tiny bit of patience which of course will be rewarded with a plateful of utter delight.

PER SERVING
30 KCAL
3G CARBS
2G PROTEIN
1G FAT

200g white cabbage, finely diced

150g chicken mince

150g pork mince

60g chestnut mushrooms, finely diced

3 spring onions, finely sliced

2.5cm fresh ginger, minced

2 cloves of garlic, minced

1 tbsp soy sauce

1 tsp sesame oil

Salt and pepper

35 gyoza wrappers

Low-calorie cooking spray

In a large bowl, combine all the ingredients except the wrappers and cooking spray using your hands. Take a wrapper and place it in the palm of your hand. Place a heaped teaspoon of filling in the centre of the wrapper. Dip your index finger into a bowl of water and draw a circle around the edge of the wrapper.

Fold the wrapper in half over the filling and pinch it in the centre with your fingers. Make 3-4 pleats using your thumb and index finger, making sure to press the folded pleat tightly against the back part of the wrapper, making sure everything is sealed nicely.

Working in batches if needed, fry the gyozas in a lidded frying pan sprayed with low-calorie cooking spray on a medium heat for 2 minutes until crispy. Add 2-3 tablespoons of water to the pan and steam with the lid on for a few minutes or until the water has evaporated.

Serve with soy sauce and dig right in!

Swaps: Use any filling you like! Go veggie by just using vegetables, or minced king prawns work amazingly well too.

SWEET TREATS

CHOCOLATE MOUSSE

 5 MINUTES　　 SERVES 3

You wouldn't believe this creamy, super indulgent chocolate mousse is made from tofu.
Every person I've taste-tested this with is in pure shock when I mention tofu, and it only
takes minutes to make!

PER SERVING
265 KCAL
2G CARBS
10G PROTEIN
15G FAT

300g silken tofu

1 tsp vanilla essence

1 tbsp liquid sweetener

100g milk chocolate, melted

15g cacao powder

Blend the tofu with the vanilla essence and liquid sweetener until smooth. Pour in the melted chocolate then sift in the cacao powder. Blend again for around 1 minute then pour into 3 ramekins.

Set the mousse in the fridge overnight and enjoy with a grating of chocolate on top and fresh fruit!

COOKIE DOUGH MUG CAKE

5 MINUTES I MINUTE SERVES I

Think of all the flavours and textures of cookie dough in a 60 second mug cake.
The easiest dessert you'll ever make.

PER SERVING
256 KCAL
40G CARBS
I2G PROTEIN
7G FAT

20g oats, blended

20g peanut butter powder

½ tsp baking powder

Pinch of salt

40ml milk

20g liquid sweetener

5g milk chocolate chips

Stir all the dry ingredients together, then mix in the milk and sweetener until smooth. Transfer the batter to a mug or ramekin and top with the chocolate chips, then microwave on high for 1 minute. Serve straight away!

Swaps: Any type of milk or flavoured liquid sweetener will do. You can use peanut butter instead of the powder but add less milk and aim for a cakey consistency.

CHOCOLATE CROISSANT PUDDING

5 MINUTES   12-14 MINUTES   SERVES 4

Think of a bread-and-butter pudding but using croissants and adding chocolate.
My work here is done.

PER SERVING
253 KCAL
25G CARBS
9G PROTEIN
13G FAT

2 eggs

75ml semi-skimmed milk

1 tbsp granulated sweetener

1 tsp vanilla essence

½ tsp ground cinnamon

4 reduced-fat croissants

40g milk chocolate, roughly chopped

Line an ovenproof dish with parchment paper. Whisk the eggs, milk, half the sweetener, the vanilla essence and cinnamon together in a jug. Slice each croissant into 4 pieces, place in the prepared dish and pour the egg mixture over them. Turn the croissant pieces in the mixture, making sure they're fully coated, then scatter the chocolate pieces in between.

Sprinkle the remaining sweetener over the top and oven cook the pudding at 180°c for 12-14 minutes or until the croissants have a nice crispy top.

Serve with low-calorie vanilla ice cream, a drizzle of milk chocolate and fresh strawberries.

Swaps: Any milk will work here, as will any type of chocolate!

CREAM CHEESE STUFFED BAKLAVA CIGARS

10 MINUTES   13-15 MINUTES   SERVES 10

A Greek classic with a twist. Inside these yummy cigar-shaped treats there's a creamy vanilla and honey centre, and they're topped with spiced pistachios over a sweet honey glaze.

PER SERVING
60 KCAL
8G CARBS
3G PROTEIN
2G FAT

2 sheets of filo pastry (54g)

15g light butter or spread, melted

100g reduced-fat soft cheese

50g fat-free Greek yoghurt

1 tsp vanilla essence

1 tsp honey

25 pistachios, crushed

1 cardamon pod, seeds crushed

½ tsp ground cinnamon

20g honey

Place both sheets of filo pastry on a chopping board, fold in half and slice twice horizontally so you have 3 even strips. Open the strips out and slice through the middle so you have 12 pieces. Set 2 aside as you only need 10 here. Brush the melted butter over each piece of filo, saving a small amount.

In a small bowl, mix the soft cheese, yoghurt, vanilla and honey together well. Place 2-3 heaped teaspoons of this filling on the far right of each filo strip, keeping it central. Fold the pastry over the filling and keep folding until there is no more pastry left. Repeat this process for all 10 cigars.

Push down the edges so the filling is tightly enclosed and place in a lined baking dish. Brush the remaining butter over the cigars and oven cook them at 180°c for 13-15 minutes, or until crispy and golden.

Meanwhile, mix the pistachios with the crushed cardamon and cinnamon. Drizzle the honey over the baked cigars, sprinkle over the pistachio topping and leave to cool before diving in.

Tips: If you like, place the finished cigars back in the oven for 1-2 minutes so the honey topping gets lovely and sticky!

APPLE CRUMBLE

5 MINUTES 22-24 MINUTES SERVES 2

A beautiful apple crumble made with a crispy oat and digestive biscuit topping. If you haven't eaten your five a day by teatime, make this dessert as it'll tick off two of them. This goes amazingly well with low-fat custard.

PER SERVING
244 KCAL
43G CARBS
4G PROTEIN
7G FAT

For the filling

3 Braeburn apples, diced

2-3 tbsp boiling water

1 tbsp maple syrup

1 tsp ground cinnamon

Squeeze of lemon juice

For the topping

40g oats

20g reduced-fat butter, melted

1 reduced-sugar digestive biscuit

In a saucepan, combine all the filling ingredients and cook on a medium heat for 3-4 minutes to soften. Transfer the apple mixture into an ovenproof dish and level out. In a separate bowl, mix the oats and melted butter together, then spread this mixture on top of the filling.

Crumble the digestive biscuit over the oats, then oven bake your crumble at 180°c for 15-20 minutes until the oats are golden brown. Serve with low-fat custard.

CARAMELISED BISCUIT CHEESECAKE

5 MINUTES   SERVES 8

My absolute favourite sweet spread of all time has got to be Biscoff. If you're anything like me, you've eaten it out the jar on one too many occasions. This cheesecake will satisfy your deepest cravings and it's so low in calories, you won't feel a bit of guilt.

PER SERVING
166 KCAL
14G CARBS
11G PROTEIN
7G FAT

For the base

40g low-fat butter or spread, melted

12 caramelised biscuits, crushed

For the filling

1 tsp gelatine powder

1 tbsp boiling water

360g reduced-fat cream cheese

300g fat-free Greek yoghurt

1 tbsp powdered sweetener

1 tsp vanilla essence

For the topping

20g caramelised biscuit spread, melted

1 caramelised biscuit, crumbled

In a bowl, combine the melted butter and biscuits for the base and then use a spatula to press the mixture down in a lined springform cake tin.

Dissolve the gelatine powder in the boiling water and then combine the liquid with all the other filling ingredients in a large bowl. Adjust the sweetener to taste, then spread the filling over the biscuit base in the tin.

Drizzle the melted spread over the cheesecake and scatter the biscuit crumbs evenly on top. Place in the fridge for at least 2 hours, or until set, and enjoy!

Tips: You don't have to use gelatine, but this keeps the filling set so your slices will be much neater!

FUDGY CHOCOLATE BROWNIES

5 MINUTES   20 MINUTES   SERVES 16

These are the fudgiest, most indulgent brownies I've ever made. To make them so low in calories, I've swapped a standard ingredient, melted chocolate, for cacao powder. But I promise you, you wouldn't even know.

PER SERVING
143 KCAL
18G CARBS
2G PROTEIN
7G FAT

115g low-fat spread, melted

1 tbsp vegetable oil

225g caster sugar

2 eggs

1 tsp vanilla essence

64g plain flour

50g cacao powder

Pinch of salt

Whisk the hot melted butter, oil and sugar together in a bowl for about a minute. Add the eggs and vanilla, then beat or whisk for another minute until the mixture is lighter in colour.

Sift the flour, cacao powder and a good pinch of salt into the bowl. Gently fold the dry ingredients into the wet until just combined.

Pour the batter into a lined brownie tin and bake in the oven at 180°c for 18-20 minutes. Remove and let the brownies cool to room temperature or leave them overnight before slicing into 16 squares. Enjoy!

Swaps: Use cocoa powder if you can't find cacao and unsalted butter instead of spread if you prefer. Stir a handful of chocolate chips into the batter for added chocolatey goodness.

MAPLE PEACH CRISP

 5 MINUTES   10 MINUTES   SERVES 2

A no-faff dessert with maple-glazed peaches, hints of cinnamon and an oat crisp topping.
Irresistible with a scoop of low-calorie vanilla ice cream.

PER SERVING
278 KCAL
48G CARBS
4G PROTEIN
7G FAT

1 tin of peach slices in natural juice,
drained

1 tbsp maple syrup

1½ tsp ground cinnamon

60g oats

Pinch of salt

1 tbsp reduced-fat butter, melted

Mix the peaches, maple syrup and 1 teaspoon of the cinnamon together in an
ovenproof dish. Blitz half the oats into flour and place in a bowl along with the
remaining oats and cinnamon. Stir in the salt and melted butter, then sprinkle
the topping over the peaches.

Oven bake at 180°c for 10-12 minutes, or until the oats are lightly browned,
and enjoy.

Tips: Cook this in the microwave for 1-2 minutes if you're short on time!

CHEAT CHURROS

10 MINUTES 10-12 MINUTES SERVES 14

Standard churros are deep-fried and calorie loaded, but my cheat version is made from just one main ingredient and oven cooked instead. The flavour is unreal, especially when they're dunked into melted chocolate!

PER SERVING
46 KCAL
6G CARBS
1G PROTEIN
3G FAT

160g ready-rolled puff pastry

Low-calorie cooking spray

25g granulated sweetener

1 tbsp ground cinnamon

Using a pizza cutter, slice the pastry in half horizontally, then cut vertically into about 14 strips. Place the strips on a lined baking tray and spray evenly with the low-calorie cooking spray.

Oven cook the pastry at 180°c for 10-12 minutes until lightly browned. Meanwhile, combine the sweetener and cinnamon in a shallow bowl. Remove the cooked pastry from the oven and spray with more low-calorie cooking spray, then carefully dip each churro into the sweet cinnamon coating. Serve with your favourite melted spreads and enjoy!

Swaps: Brush the churros with melted reduced-fat spread instead of the cooking spray once they're out of the oven for extra indulgence.

SNICKERS BANANA BOATS

This might be the easiest dessert you will ever make and just needs five ingredients. I always make a double batch and keep them in my freezer to bring out for guests. Fresh banana 'boats' are layered with peanut butter, caramel, crunchy peanuts and of course an indulgent chocolate coating.

PER SERVING
100 KCAL
11G CARBS
2G PROTEIN
6G FAT

3 ripe bananas, peeled

60g reduced-fat smooth peanut butter

45g caramel drizzle or sauce

30g peanuts, crushed

60g milk chocolate, melted

Slice the bananas in half lengthways, then slice again widthways to get 4 pieces per banana. Spread a thin layer of peanut butter over each piece, then add the caramel, sprinkle with crushed peanuts and finish with a drizzle of melted chocolate.

Place on a lined baking tray with a pinch of sea salt on top and leave in the fridge to set, or store them in the freezer for a rainy day!

Tips: Caramel drizzle works best for this recipe but if you can't find any, heat up caramel sauce to get the right consistency for drizzling or just spread it over.

STICKY TOFFEE PUDDING

5 MINUTES   14-16 MINUTES   SERVES 4

Who can resist this luxurious dessert? The sponge is light but moreish and soaks up the toffee sauce wonderfully. This recipe has everything you need in a sticky toffee pudding but it's ridiculously low in calories, and the best part is that it only takes 20 minutes to make.

PER SERVING
235 KCAL
30G CARBS
4G PROTEIN
11G FAT

For the pudding

50g low-fat butter or Stork, melted

50g light brown sugar

1 egg

50g self-raising flour

¼ tsp baking powder

¼ tsp bicarbonate of soda

For the sauce

50g caramel sauce

1 tsp black treacle

40ml milk

Put the melted butter, brown sugar and egg into a large bowl and mix until combined. Stir in the rest of the ingredients until a smooth, thick batter has formed and then pour this into a small lined baking dish. Oven cook at 200°c for 14-16 minutes.

Using a toothpick or skewer, pierce the baked pudding multiple times and then set aside. Combine the sauce ingredients in a small pan on a low heat and mix well for a few minutes, then pour the sauce over the pudding.

Serve with a scoop of vanilla ice cream, and make more sauce to pour over the top for extra indulgence if you like.

Tips: Any milk would work in this recipe and you could make your own caramel sauce, but be aware of the calories!

CINNAMON ROLLS

5-10 MINUTES   14-16 MINUTES   SERVES 15

These sweet cinnamon swirls are absolute joy and I highly doubt you'll only be eating the one.
You won't need to wait around for them to rise either, as no yeast is needed in the magical
two-ingredient dough, so they'll be the quickest cinnamon rolls you've ever made.

PER SERVING
60 KCAL
1G CARBS
3G PROTEIN
1G FAT

180g low-fat Greek yoghurt

180g self-raising flour

10g light butter or spread, melted

2-3 tbsp granulated sweetener

1 tbsp ground cinnamon

Low-calorie cooking spray

30g icing sugar

15g low-fat Greek yoghurt

In a bowl, mix the yoghurt and flour together until a dough forms. Using a floured rolling pin, roll out the dough on a floured surface to a rectangle shape, around the thickness of a pound coin.

In a small bowl, combine the sweetener and cinnamon. (If you have a sweet tooth like me, use the full 3 tablespoons). Brush the melted butter over the dough, then evenly sprinkle on the cinnamon topping, rubbing it in using your hands.

Tightly roll up the dough rectangle starting from the side nearest to you, then place seam-side down making sure to seal the edges together. Slice the roll into 15 equal pieces, then place in a cake or pie dish sprayed with low-calorie cooking spray.

Oven bake the cinnamon rolls at 180°c for 14-16 minutes or until lightly golden and cooked through. Allow them to cool for 5 minutes before mixing the icing sugar and Greek yoghurt together to drizzle over the rolls.

Tips: You can make about 8 bigger rolls with this recipe if preferred, but make sure to bake them for 20-25 minutes.

TIRAMISU

I made this indulgent coffee-flavoured dessert so light by switching the mascarpone cheese for thick vanilla-flavoured Greek yoghurt. But I didn't forget the cream and a dusting of cocoa powder to bring this Italian classic to life!

PER SERVING
125 KCAL
17G CARBS
10G PROTEIN
2G FAT

4 trifle sponges

1 tsp coffee granules

50ml boiling water

300g fat-free Greek yoghurt

1 tbsp powdered sweetener

1 tsp vanilla essence

12.5g light squirty cream

5g cacao or cocoa power

Slice the trifle sponges horizontally through the middle so you've got 8 flat pieces, then place 4 of these in a dish. Make up the coffee by dissolving the granules in the boiling water in a mug or bowl.

Spoon 1 tablespoon of coffee at a time over the sponges in the dish, coating them but making sure they don't get too soggy. In a separate bowl, combine the yoghurt with the sweetener and vanilla essence until well mixed, then spoon half of this on top of the sponge layer.

Place the remaining 4 sponge pieces on top of the vanilla yoghurt, soak them in the remaining coffee and then cover with the remaining vanilla yoghurt.

Add the whipped cream, then sift the cacao or cocoa powder over your tiramisu and enjoy!

Tips: If you prefer a stronger coffee flavour, use a heaped teaspoon of coffee granules. This recipe works incredibly well with shop-bought fat-free vanilla yoghurt too!

MILLIONAIRE'S SHORTBREAD

5 MINUTES   30 MINUTES   SERVES 16

A delicious treat made in no time with only five ingredients. The shortbread layer is so delicious that I sometimes just make it by itself, it's that good! But the caramel sauce and chocolate layer are just the cherry on the cake.

PER SERVING
115 KCAL
17G CARBS
2G PROTEIN
5G FAT

130g plain flour

50g caster sugar sweetener

85g light butter or spread

160g caramel

100g milk chocolate, melted

Pinch of sea salt (optional)

Put the flour, sweetener and butter in a large bowl and use your hands to combine the mixture until it resembles breadcrumbs. Using a spatula, transfer to a square brownie tin and press down well using your hands.

Oven cook the shortbread base at 160°c for 30 minutes, then leave to cool for 10 minutes before spreading the caramel over the top.

Drizzle the melted chocolate over the caramel layer and spread out evenly with a spatula. If you like, sprinkle sea salt over the top to taste. Place in the freezer for at least 30 minutes or until set and then slice into 16 squares to serve.

ACKNOWLEDGEMENTS

I couldn't have written this book or be where I am today without the huge support from my incredible, and I mean incredible, social media community. From the moment I shared my first recipe, to seeing all your wonderful re-creations, you have been there from the very beginning and I couldn't have done it without you.

My grandparents always told me to make my dreams a reality and never stop until I get there. Watching them cook through my childhood, seeing the passion and love they put into their food and life, made me who I am today. They are my inspiration.

A big thank you to all my friends who supported me, especially through the months where I was flat out getting the book ready while juggling two jobs, three social media platforms and life. To them, it seemed like I had fallen off the face of the earth. You are the best friends I could ever ask for.

And lastly, big thanks to you, the reader, for buying my book and for believing in me and my recipes.

Thank you.